FIRST LADY SPY *of* INA

Neera Arya

FIRST LADY SPY *of* INA

Neera Arya

MADHU DHAMA

Published by

PRABHAT PRAKASHAN PVT. LTD.
4/19 Asaf Ali Road,
New Delhi-110002 (INDIA)
e-mail: prabhatbooks@gmail.com

ISBN 978-93-5488-662-1
FIRST LADY SPY OF INA: NEERA ARYA
by Madhu Dhama

Sketch by Sumit Sharma
Cover photo: Aryakhand

Edition
2025

Price
₹ 300 (Rupees Three Hundred Only)

Printed at
R-Tech Offset Printers, Delhi

Foreword by Chandra Prakash Dwivedi

The 'First Lady Spy of INA – Neera Arya' is a heart wrenching saga of the untold heroes of our Nation. Madhu Dhama's account of Neera Arya's journey, brings life to the sacrifices made by this valiant woman so, as a nation, we are reaping the benefits of Independence.

Author's Note

When I first met Neera Arya, her hut was getting demolished by the Hyderabad Municipal Corporation. It was built on the government land. But the Hyderabad Municipal Corporation officials did not know that they were pulling down the hut of a great freedom fighter.

Once when we wanted to help Neera Arya, she shared with us the address of Saraswati Rajamani and told us to help her instead. Saraswati Rajamani had lost a leg in the freedom struggle. She also motivated us to help Colonel Nizamuddin but did not accept any help for herself. In those days, just like Neera, no one knew Colonel Nizamuddin and Saraswati Rajamani.

Once, we had asked Neera ji, 'Amma, who arrested you?' Her answer was, 'George VI and Lady Elizabeth Bowes-Lyon's pet dog Brigadier J. A. Salomons.'

Neera used to say that the Indian soldiers working in the British Army were denied all kinds of information related to the British. The proof is that the Indian soldiers who served the British used to say on every point - thank Queen Victoria, while Queen Victoria died on January 22, 1901. The rulers were George VI and Lady Elizabeth Bowes-Lyon.

Neera writes in her diary that under the supervision of a military doctor and warden of Agra Jail, J.P. Walker and jailer David Berry, the first batch of revolutionaries reached Kala Pani in a small warship on March 10, 1858. When the first group of prisoners arrived, there was only rocky and lifeless land to welcome them and forests with dense and sky-high trees, which would not allow even the sunbeam to pass and reach the earth. Open blue sky, toxic climate, severe water crisis and tribes armed with arrows ready to kill humans at first sight.

When some British officers found Kala Pani a fun place, they planned debauchery. Women prisoners from Madras, Bengal, Bombay, North West States, Awadh, Punjab, etc., who had spent a few years in the jails of British India, were being sent to Kala Pani for the pleasure of the British officers. Women prisoners who served no use to the British officers were married off to male prisoners. In 1897, out of 2447 self-supporters, 363 were women.

With time, a moment came in history when Netaji Subhas hoisted the tricolour in Kala Pani. But after the end of World War II in 1945, the British again captured it. Subsequently, Brigadier J. A. Salomons locked hundreds of queens of the Rani Jhansi Regiment in the dungeon of Kala Pani. And then, the women imprisoned in Kala Pani were not only subjected to mental and physical abuse till independence but all limits of sexual abuse were also crossed. Neera Arya was also one of those oppressed women who endured the torture at Kala Pani. While leaving, the British took those documents of Kala Pani with them, in which the details of the Kala Pani punishment of anonymous women of the Rani Jhansi Regiment were recorded. The French writer Dominique Lapierre once met us in Hyderabad. He wanted to get done a simple Hindi version of *Freedom at Midnight*. He said that in the documents based on which he has written *Freedom at Midnight*, there is evidence of severe torture in Kala Pani given to the prisoners of the Rani Jhansi Regiment. Dominique Lapierre got the simple Hindi version of Freedom at Midnight done by us.

It is believed that no prisoner ever escaped from Kala Pani. But Dominique Lapierre writes that the prisoners named Mehtab and Chetan escaped from Kala Pani on March 26, 1872. They travelled 750 miles across the Bay of Bengal in a boat made by them. Taking inspiration from Mehtab and Chetan, Neera Arya was the only female prisoner who managed to escape from Kala Pani.

– Madhu Dhama

– Tejpal Singh Dhama

Contents

1.

Scorching heat of June! A stony path surfaced with pointed pebbles and shadowy trees, not even a blade of green grass was visible on that long and less trodden path. Only thorny bushes were companions of the path, which I used to tread every day on foot. This was the route from the railway station which led to my house. There was a government school on the way and there was a dilapidated hut of an old woman by the outer wall of the school complex. We used to see each other daily and I would exchange smiles with her. I saw her making garlands of flowers daily and many women bought flowers from her for their braids. Often, I also had the craving to buy flowers and adorn my braid, but my principles and upbringing didn't allow me to wear flowers in my bun or to adorn and flaunt my assets.

But the fact was that whenever I stepped out of my house, I had a burqa on, covering my body from head to toe with a black cloak, which even had a nose piece in front of the eyes and as soon as I entered the house, I slipped out of my burqa. In the house, I was busy with household chores and homework from the school, and then, where was the time to adorn and, who was there for whom I should adorn myself? But during those days, I liked someone, whom I used to meet outside the house. Please don't take it otherwise, the person whom I loved, was none other than my fiancé[1] and our relationship had the blessings of my father. I was hardly seventeen, when I was betrothed to a stranger, who belonged to a distant far away land and not much was known to my family about him.

I have recorded all these things in my biography 'Ghar Vapsi', 'Dar Dar ki Thokren' and book of reminiscences, 'Mera Doosra Janma', but here I am writing about that old lady whom I used to meet daily. That day, when I passed by her hut, I found that the Municipal Committee had razed it and thrown her belongings which were scattered on the road. She didn't have many belongings and whatever she had, lay littered on the road, that included a few earthen pots, one blanket and one or two ragged clothes. But, yes, there were some more important things in her belongings and those were her books, diaries and documents. She made an appeal to the policemen showing them those documents, "Who do you think I am? Had we ousted the British from the country, so that you should take over their role?"

Taken aback by her claims, I wondered as to how an illiterate appearing old lady, who made both ends meet by selling flowers, could talk of the freedom struggle and, then looked at the books littered on the road. None of those were a story book or a novel, but all were related to history of the freedom struggle and to me, those appeared to be rare books. I picked up a book, which was *Sun 42 ka Mahan Viplav*. (The Great Uprising of '42), which contained shocking narrations and pictures. I had asked the lady, "Amma, are you a freedom fighter?"

"Beti (daughter), I am an ordinary citizen."

"Was anybody from your family a freedom fighter?"

"Why are you asking me all this?" she said. "What does it matter who is who these days?"

"Looking at your books, it appears that you are not an ordinary citizen. You are hiding your identity from people and selling flowers to earn your livelihood."

"Yes, beti, I am hiding my dignity from people, otherwise how would this wretched world allow a single woman to survive? I am hiding my poverty from the world that is why I bless every married woman by selling flowers for her braid, so that my flowers continue to be sold."

"Amma, you have avoided my question...these books littered on the road are telling a different story. These prove one thing for certain that you are a literate lady and secondly, you are a patriot."

"Don't add insult to my injuries," she started weeping, "tell these policemen not to ruin my abode."

A policeman interfered, "Ammagaru, you have been warned repeatedly not to occupy the road, move to some other place. We had also made arrangement for you at an old age home, but you have repeatedly refused to shift there and all the time you have been pleading that you don't want charity from the government and that you are capable of looking after yourself."

"I am still able to look after myself, then why was my hut destroyed?"

"Because it is illegal."

"Look, son, It was a vast jungle, when I made my hut here. I had made my home outside the city, but now in its development process, the city has surged ahead of me. It is not my fault."

"Amma, which period are you talking of?'

"I came here in 1947, when this land belonged to the Nizam government. Gone are the days of the Nizam's rule, now it is our own rule and as such this is our land, then why am I not being allowed to live here?"

Well then, how long could I have stayed there, I left for my home..the old lady had looked at me with eyes filled with hope. Next day, when I passed that side, I found her lying at the roadside. It had rained heavily at night and she had been lying drenched in the rains. Her luggage was littered on the road, but her books were not there, which might have been taken by a junk dealer. Silently, I approached her and placed my hand on her forehead and I was shocked, it was very warm. She had high fever. I called her, "Amma...Amma... Amm..." but there was no response from her, as she was unconscious.

For a moment, I thought, "what is she to me, she doesn't belong to my caste or community, she doesn't believe in my faith and belief...she is a Hindu...she is an infidel...why should I have sympathy for her? How am I concerned with her? If she dies or lives, I am not bothered. The sooner these infidels leave the world, the better it would be, so that the world is ruled by Allah, let the sharia be imposed and all the people are turned into followers of Islam. Suddenly, there was another voice from my inner heart. "What is a Hindu or a Muslim? All of them are humans. There is no religion of an ailing old lady, there is no God, his or her religion is the treatment and his or her God is the doctor and one who helps the destitute and helpless is a prophet." The moment such thoughts struck my mind, I took out a mobile phone from my pocket, those days Reliance had brought out cheaper mobiles in the market. This phone was gifted to me by my fiancé. He was madly in love with me, but I used to ignore his overtures and had told him, "All these things after marriage, just keep yourself limited to blinking. In fact, I was unaware of the proceedings after marriage."

I called him, "Amma is unconscious."

"Amma! Who?" He asked, as I used to call my mother Ammi and I didn't know his mother.

"Oh! That, flower-seller Amma, from whom you used to buy flowers for me."

"Then, how am I concerned? I am not a doctor."

"That is what I am telling you, she is to be taken to a doctor."

"To a doctor?" He replied, "What is she to me? Why should I take her to a doctor?"

"She will die, without treatment."

"Let her die, am I responsible for providing treatment to orphans?"

"How can people love their own ones, if they have no sympathy for destitute, orphans and ill people?" I was enraged. "I hate you mister, you ungrateful lover!" I had disconnected the phone.

I waited on the road for a rickshaw, but there was not a single rickshaw in sight that day as if all of them were on strike. The rickshaw stand was also far away. I was worried, if Amma was not taken to a hospital immediately, she would die and in that condition, I would be responsible for that sin. I put my bag on my shoulder and tried to lift Amma with both hands. I thought that I would take her to the hospital lifting her in my lap. How much weight would this old lady have, but I was not that strong..I was just a frail girl. Even then, I was able to lift her but there was strain in my back and suddenly I felt a shooting pain. At that moment, I saw a rickshaw approaching me, and a person was sitting in that rickshaw. I thought of requesting the passenger to let me use the rickshaw for taking the ailing lady to the hospital. But as the rickshaw approached, I recognized the person who was none other than my fiancé. He was ashamed of his behavior and had come to my help. Alighting from the rickshaw without uttering a word, he took the lady in his lap and sat in the rickshaw and asked the rickshaw-puller to take him to the nearest hospital. Then he turned to me and said, "Darling, you follow us on foot." He was behaving as if he was settling a score with me. But the robust butcher-like rickshaw-puller took pity on me and said, "come, madam, you also come along with us, I'll take three passengers and would earn a little more." Then turning back, he asked my fiancé, "Sir, why are you taking bread out of my mouth? Let the madam also come with us."

I blinked at my lover and immediately alighted the rickshaw and nudged him, but he was unable to respond as he was carrying the old lady in his lap, he could only grit his teeth, "You, shameless creature!"

Finally, we got Amma admitted to a hospital and he stayed there with Amma and I left for my home. He stayed there the whole night. Next day, I reached the hospital early in the morning and asked him, "How is Amma?"

"She has gained consciousness and just gone to sleep." As he was telling me about her condition, Amma woke up and said, "So you have come Beti... how could I sleep? Now I have to go to eternal sleep..." turning towards my fiancé, she said, "I have to go to the toilet."

Then again she said, “Please make haste or I will spoil my clothes.”

I tried to lift her, but the old lady said, “Son, I am too weak to walk and this girl is too frail to lift me, please help me and take me to the toilet.”

“But, how can I take you to the ladies toilet?”

“You had called me mother, then why do you feel ashamed in taking your mother to the toilet?”

“It’s not that, mother. There is nothing to be ashamed of.”

Both of us took her to the toilet. After we entered, my fiancé, immediately went outside and gathered her clothes, I made her sit on the toilet seat.

She neither urinated nor excreted, she just got up and said, “Take me out.” I called him and both of us took her back to the bed. After lying down, she looked at me tenderly and said, “How will I be able to repay your debt?”

“Debt! You are embarrassing me?” Then I said, “Will you oblige me, Amma?”

“Tell me. beti.” Then she said, “Do you want to leave me alone here? If it is so, then go.”

“No, Amma. It is not so. We will leave only when you are fully treated.” I said, “I just want to know about your past. I had seen a number of revolutionary books among your belongings, which lead me to believe that you are not an ordinary human being.”

“Beti! You want to know my past. It is the past, which never leaves a person and follows them to their grave..” Moments after Amma had travelled back to her past and her face had turned child-like...

❑

2.

"Help!...help!...help!..." drowning in the sea, I was shouting but people ashore were mute observers, none of them had come forward to the help of a drowning girl. I was just an adolescent those days.

Suddenly, a young man dived into the sea and made his way through the waves. Fighting with the strong current, he approached me and took me out of the water. He made me lie down on my stomach and pumped the saline water out of me. Within a few moments, I regained consciousness. "Brother!" I said to him, "I'll remain grateful till my last breath for saving my life, one day I'll repay for this debt."[2]

"When you have called me your brother, then how can there be a debt for a sister?" He said, "It is Rakshabandan today, come tie a rakhi on the wrist of this brother."

I got up but I didn't have a rakhi at that time. I thought for a moment and plucked out few strands of my hair and tied them on his wrist, I said, "Brother, I have tied the rakhi, regard these as silk threads."

"I am honoured, sister!" Then he asked me, "What is your name? And when you don't know swimming, why did you go into the sea?"

"Brother, I am Neera and I know swimming, but never had a chance to swim in a sea. There is a small canal in our village, where along with friends, I enjoyed swimming."

"What is the name of your village?"

"Khekra is the name of my village."

"Where is this Khekra?"

"Have you heard about Meerut?"

"Meerut, the sacred land of Mangal Pandey!" The young man said, "Who can forget Meerut, where the first freedom struggle took place and the torch of that struggle is still glowing and it would remain burning till our country does not attain independence."

"I am a resident of that Khekra village, which is nearer to Delhi than Meerut."

"How is it that you have come so far?"

"My godfather, Seth Chhajjumal is a trader and he has come to Calcutta in connection with his business. He was busy at a meeting with a party for finalizing a deal and I along with a servant, came here to enjoy swimming. The servant has gone somewhere leaving me alone here, so I decided to swim. It was just my misfortune that I couldn't keep my balance against a powerful wave and started drowning, but luckily you were there and you saved my life. Who are you, brother?"

"Sister, my name is Subhas Chandra Bose," he said, "Come, let me take you to your father."

"Leave it brother, I'll go on my own."

❑

3.

With its own speed, time passed. I still remember the day, when my godfather took me to Calcutta for the first time, then my mother, Dhakhan Devi had taken me in her lap and asked, "Where were you till now?" Listening to these words, I turned into a protected person or entity from an orphan. My brother Basant also embraced the mother. Then casting an inquisitive glance, he asked me, "Didi (elder sister), is she our Lakshmi mother?"

"Yes, I am your Lakshmi Mother." And from that day Mai Dankhan Devi became Lakshmi. My godfather Chhajjumal also started calling her Lakshmi. May be it was the first time in history that children had given a name to their guardian mother and that too by children who were not born to her.

We spent our childhood at the bungalow at Central Avenue in Calcutta. My godbrother, Sajjan Kumar had great affection for me. He loved me more that his own sister Savitri and I too took good care of him. Later, after marriage he brought Komal Bhabhi for me, I had stopped them at the door-step as a ritual, under which both of them were allowed entry to the house only after giving me a gift. The real name of Komal

Bhabhi was Komola Beg. Her brother was known as Tara Ali Beg. They had converted to the Vedic religion.

My godfather was a nationalist and he wanted us to be nationalists too. He did not send my younger sister, Savitri to the missionary school, but asked Jalandhar Girls School to send a lady teacher to our house to teach my younger sister at our house and also to inculcate nationalist feelings in her. So the Headmistress of the school asked a teacher of her school, Sushila to resign and sent her to our house. Sushila was young and my godfather was astonished to meet her. But when he asked a few questions, he was so impressed with her knowledge that he bowed before her. Sushila and I had our birthdays on 5th March and our birthdays were celebrated together in the house. I was older than Sushila by three years, so she used to call me Didi but there were many persons for whom she was a Didi. Thus, I was an elder sister to an elder one.

On December 17, 1928, Sushila got a telegram that a certain Durgawati was coming to meet her, but she failed to recognize who this Durgawati was, still he reached the station and only then she came to know that her brother and bhabhi were coming with a baby. Seeing him, mother immediately recognized him. He was, in fact, revolutionary Bhagat Singh. He himself had wired Sushila, so that she could come to the station. Bhagat Singh had intentionally written Durgawati, instead of Durga Bhabhi to avoid intelligence personnel. I was told later that it was Sushila, who had started calling Durga Bhabhi.

"Mother, when you have recognized me, then do you have any objection to my staying here with you?" Bhagat Singh had asked my mother, to which she replied, "I give my word, that you will stay here like my Sajjan."

Then she went to the kitchen to prepare food for Bhagat Singh. An upper floor room was prepared for Bhagat Singh to stay.

One day, Bhagat Singh was standing at the balcony and was looking at the road, where a hawker milkman, Ramdhan Bihari was selling milk. Jokingly, I asked, "Bhagat Bhaiya, how much milk can you drink at a time?"

He said, "As much as you say."

"Can you drink vendor's whole milk?"

"Listen Neera, make the sea as a cup and fill it with milk, I will drink all that, you know I am a descendant of Agastya Muni!"

Immediately, I went downstairs and came back with Ramdhan, who had brought milk in a pail. The price was negotiated and Bhagat Bhai gave a rupee to the milkman and drank all the milk in the pail.

The milkman stared in disbelief at Bhagat's face, but he had no choice but to leave the place.

Newspapers of the next day carried a photo of Bhagat Singh, which was also seen by the milkman. Immediately, he came to our house and putting the rupee in Bhagat Singh's hand, he started weeping, "Babuji, you are Bhagat Singh, why didn't you tell me earlier? Please take back this rupee, then only will I feel that I have done some service to the country." Forcibly, he put the rupee in Bhaiya's pocket, but then the armed police surrounded our bungalow. We thought the milkman was an informer of the Police.

Now, Bhagat Singh decided to show the Police, how a revolutionary could fight with the Police. He loaded his revolver and took his position. He was standing firmly at the door to the stairs but Sushila removed and I pushed him into the room. Sushila said, “Impatience is not advisable, just have patience. Let us see, why the Police have come?”

We came outside and after enquiry, we realized that it was a different matter. Police were looking for the famous Arya Samaji leader who had been staying in our house, Bhawani Dayal Sanyasi, who was accused of making a speech against the government.

The police went back after arresting Swami Bhawani Dayal from the first floor of the house. The crisis was diffused.

❑

4.

I, the adolescent of yesterday had turned into a youthful woman and went to my in-laws' house after my marriage to Srikant Jairanjan Das. Srikant was a senior officer in the Intelligence Department. He was instrumental in getting a number of revolutionaries arrested. Earlier, he was sent to Afghanistan to spy on Raja Mahendra, but later he was entrusted the task of spying on Netaji. Netaji was the same person who had saved my life. So, when my husband, set forth for his mission of spying on Subhas Bose and if possible killing him, I asked him, "Are you aware of what you are going to do?"

"What I am going to do?" Srikant told me, "I am spying against a traitor and if possible I am going to kill him. Do you know how much money will be given to me as a reward, if I succeed in killing him?"

"How much?" I asked sarcastically.

"Two lakhs of rupees!" excited Srikant replied, "This is such a huge sum of money that our next seven generations will enjoy the fruits of life."

"And what about those thousands of generations, who would curse you?" Seriously I asked him, "Why don't you resign from the government job? What is the use of such a service, where one is forced to work against one's own people?"

"I am not working against my own people, but I am working against traitors and terrorists."

"Traitors!" I was blind with rage, "Those, whom you call traitors or terrorists are patriots, great! patriots."

"They, and patriots! They are traitors of Queen Victoria!" A crooked smile spread across his face.

"Tell me, Srikant." I asked her seriously, "You want two lakhs of rupees or your wife, Neera?"

"May I ask, why you have such sympathy towards Subhas?"

"Because, he is my brother."

"Subhas and your brother? I can't believe this."

"He had saved my life." And then I narrated to him the whole story.

"But today, he is a traitor. Is it right to sympathise with such a brother?"

"Not he, but you are the enemy of the nation." I said, "I am asking you to choose between, government service or your wife."

"Then let it be the government service! There is no dearth of women, I'll get another one, but money and honour may not come by my side again."

"All right, then I am going back to my father's house," and I started packing.[3]

❑

5.

Though Netaji Subhas Chandra Bose had been put under house arrest for his revolutionary activities, yet befooling the British and disguised as a Maulana, he succeeded in fleeing from the house and reached Peshawar, the capital of the north-west border province."

The news of Subhas fleeing came as a surprise for the British government, who immediately ordered Srikant and other British intelligence officers, "Kill Netaji Subhas at sight. In case he seeks help from Japan or Germany, kill him immediately, as Subhas has turned the biggest threat to Britain. Subhas might be trying to reach Germany via the Middle East, he mustn't be allowed to reach there and must be liquidated on his way."

But the British intelligence officers were worried about his whereabouts. Where could he go, after his disappearance in January 1941? These Intelligence officers thought that Netaji must have headed towards the Far East, but they got information from Italy about his being in Kabul and he is trying to reach Germany via the Middle East. Then, two agents posted in Turkey were directed from the London Headquarters to kill

Subhas before he reached Germany. But, the agents failed to locate him, as it was impossible to recognize him in his new disguise.

Meanwhile, Subhas reached Peshawar. He had boarded the Frontier Mail at Gomo station. He met one of his colleagues, Mian Akbar Shah of the Forward Block. Akbar Shah took him to Bhagat Ram Talwar of the Kirti Kisan Party. From Peshawar, Subhas Babu and Talwar headed for Kabul, the capital of Afghanistan. In this journey, Talwar was disguised as a Pathan, Rehmat Khan, whereas Subhas Babu had become his deaf and dumb uncle. They completed this journey on foot through the hills.

In Kabul, Subhas Babu stayed with an Indian trader, Uttam Chandra Malhotra for two months. There he tried to seek entry into the Russian Embassy. Having failed, he tried to contact the German and Italian Embassies. With the Italian Embassy his efforts bore fruits. The German and Italian Embassies helped him. Ultimately, disguised as an Italian, Hollando Matsuta, Subhas Babu reached Berlin, the capital of Germany from Kabul by train via Russian capital Moscow.

In Nazi Germany, the first person whom Subhas met, was Ribbentrop. Later, a German Minister, Adam von Trott became a close friend of Subhas Babu, who was the in-charge of Indian Affairs Department in German Foreign Office and he was assisted by Alexender Worth. Von Trotrt was always cooperative to Subhas Babu. Had he not helped Subhas in his mission, Subhas would not have been able to carry the task of directing the Indian freedom struggle successfully from a foreign land.

In Berlin, Subhas was kept at Sophienstraße , where an American Military Attaché had been residing. Subhas was feeling a whole world of difference between officials of British Empire and that of German government officials. None of the German officials ever treated Subhas with apprehension, disdain or contempt. He was a great revolutionary from India, as such, the German officials carried a great respect for him. All high officials in Berlin had been very liberal towards Subhas Chandra Bose.

It was May 29, 1942, when Subhas Babu met the supreme German Leader, Adolf Hitler. First, Subhas Chandra Bose was seated in a room. After a while, a man came to him extending his hand, he said, "I am Hitler.."

Subhas also extended his hand and said, "I am Subhas from India...but you are not Hitler."

"Then, who am I?"

"You are Harishchandra Vidyarthi, son of Swami Shradhanand."

In fact, Hitler had enlisted few lookalikes as his bodyguards, who looked like Hitler. These guards included Swami Shradhanand's son, Harishchandra, who was with Hitler those days. It was very difficult to identify Harishchandra, whether he was an Indian or Hitler.

Subhas had identified him rightly. When another person entered the room, he also extended his hand and said, "I am Hitler."

Subhas again shook hands with him and said, "I am Subhas from India...you too, can't be Hitler...I have come here to meet Hitler only. Please don't waste my time."

The third time also, another person with exactly the same appearance entered the room and stood before him. This time,

Subhas said, "I am Subhas...I have come from India, but before we shake hands, please pull out your gloves, as I don't want any kind of wall between friendship."

Hitler was considered to be a harsh person. A few people could take courage of speaking like this before him. Listening to the courageous talks of Subhas and looking at his radiant face, it was for the first time, Hitler took out his gloves and shook hands with Subhas and that was the moment when a great friendship developed between the two.

But, how did Subhas recognize the real Hitler? The fact was that both of them came to the room and extended their hands saying, "I am Hitler", but whenever a person visits another person, then the visitor extends his hand first in greeting...introduces oneself, but here the host was extending his hand first. This is the usual formality, which is observed. Third time, when Hitler himself came, he silently stood before Subhas. Subhas introduced himself...extended his hand and said, "I am Subhas." In his autobiography, Mein Kampf Hitler had criticized India and Indians. During the meeting, Subhas Babu expressed his displeasure over this. Hitler was apologetic about this and promised to delete this chapter in his next version of Mein Kampf. Till then, the world was unknown about Subhas' journey to Germany and his meeting with Hitler.

❑

6.

Subhas was not the only Indian in Germany during those days, there were thousands of Indians, but they were not ordinary citizens, but were prisoners of war. In early October 1941, *The Gemp* weekly, a publication for war prisoners, reported, "after dodging British jail authorities, Subhas is likely to reach Germany." Not many gave credence to this news, as military officials had a limited level of understanding, and secondly, all of them were greatly influenced by the British. It was concluded that the story had been planted by the Germans with an ulterior motive. But some sensible persons trusted the news, as the truth was soon going to be revealed.

During the morning roll call of October 18, 1941, an announcement was made that the great leader, Subhas Chandra Bose would be addressing them on 20th October. On hearing the announcement, prisoners were overjoyed, but some of them felt offended and they started conspiring against him. There were about 8,000 prisoners at that time. During the night, a resident of Kharad village of Rohtak, Risaldar Major Shish Ram, who later became captain, called a meeting of the officers, "We have come to know that Netaji Subhas

Chandra Bose has arrived in Germany," he continued, "this is fortunate for our country and we must support him."

"But this could be a false news," said Chaudhary Dal Singh.

"No, this is not a false news"

"Let us see." He said, "May be this will turn out to be a true news."

There was a Doctor Bose among the prisoners, who knew Netaji well, said, "If I found that he is the real Subhas Chnadra Bose, I'll give a positive signal, otherwise a negative signal would be given."

"All right, we shall await your signal." Shish Ram said, "We shall enter the lecture hall only on your positive indication, otherwise we shall refuse to go there."

Arrangements for two large halls were made outside the camp for prisoners and they were asked to assemble there before the arrival of Subhas Chandra Bose. At the appointed time, in a convoy of hundreds of vehicles and along with high German officers, high officials and a battery of press, Subhas Chandra Bose arrived there. With a guard of honour, he entered the hall. All eyes were focused on Subhas Bose, and as per planned conspiracy, some people started talking or coughing, creating a disturbance in the proceedings, but there were many sensible prisoners, who were attentive to his speech.

"My dear countrymen! I am sad that you are being held as prisoners in a foreign land. You have been lured by monetary benefits to a foreign land for enslaving others, whereas you yourselves are slaves. You can very well understand the difficulties I had to face to free myself from the clutches of the

British and the hazardous journeys I had to take. It's a long story, which is not relevant here. My sole aim is to liberate Mother India and this would only be possible when you are prepared to sacrifice your lives in pursuance of this mission. I would like to have only those of you who are willing to participate in this freedom struggle, at the cost of their lives. I assure you of freedom and this is not a hollow promise. After independence, an Indian would be the chief commanding officer and the entire administration including Governor, magistrates, DA and SP, would be in the hands of Indians. Germans are enemies of our enemy. British are our enemies and Germans are enemies of the British, as such we must strive for the liberation of Mother India with the help of the enemies of our enemy.

"Germany is a conqueror today and all odds are favouring them. Hitler and Berlin have become household names. I can't proclaim the result of this world war, but, I can assure you of one thing, that the British would be ousted, they won't remain in India. Give your blood and liberate Mother India."

War-prisoners decided to support Netaji's war for freedom. Next day, Subhas Chandra Bose was scheduled to visit the camp. But Risaldar Major conspired against his visit and issued orders, "All the prisoners would remain in their barracks and nobody would come out during Netaji's visit."

At night, Chaudhary Dal Singh and others decided to support Netaji. They called a meeting at the gurudwara (a place for meetings in the camp) and decided, "Netaji should be received at the gate."

The German Camp Commander was informed of the decision, so that Risaldar Major could be stopped in creating any kind of obstruction. As per the plan, Dal Singh and a number of soldiers came out of their barracks at 9.30 in the morning and Risaldar Major approached them and told them that they were not to go to receive Netaji and must return to their barracks. But they didn't listen to his advice and gathered at the gate. Following them, Risaldar Major himself came to the gate to ask them to go back, but was stopped by a German Officer and he had to apologise and return back.

Surrounded by German Offiicials, press reporters, photographers and security personnel, Netaji arrived at the gate in a convoy of cars. The war prisoners shouted slogans like 'long live Subhas Chandra Bose' and 'long live Gandhi and Nehru'. On hearing slogans, all the emotionally-charged inmates of the camp came out and prostrated before him on the ground. Netaji applauded and encouraged them. Photographers clicked hundreds of photographs. It was such an emotional meeting and it appeared that the prisoners were repenting their earlier mistakes.

Bose Babu briefly addressed them and at the end, he told them, "I have asked the Camp Commander to look after the prisoners well."

Next day, a workshop was started, where minor repair work could be carried out. Barbers were supplied with implements for regular shaving of the prisoners and money was provided for purchase of daily use items. Prisoners were introduced to Netaji at night and it was decided to form an Indian military force in Germany and four persons were appointed to enlist prisoners for this force.

On Netaji's arrival in Germany, the Indian Military force was formed. Its headquarters was established at Berlin and its Military Headquarters was located at Kuniesberg, where fifty Indian students and some citizens had done some work before the onset of the Second World War. The four prisoners, who had been sent to Germany from Sicily, were also sent to this camp. Necessary arrangements were made for broadcasting of news from Kuniesberg to India. Such news was broadcast on Azad Hind Radio. Prisoners, who were sent for working in the camps at Kuniesberg, were allowed to buy goods from the government canteen. They were provided with ration and other essential articles in sufficient quantity. In addition to this, through inspirational lectures and other activities, they were inspired to love India and hate the British and an environment was created, where they could be encouraged to join the Indian Military Force. This led the prisoners voluntarily enlisting themselves to this force. Those, who refused to join the Force, were transferred to another camp in France. For one year, there was no information about those, who were deputed for the task. No one knew, where they were or what happened to them and nobody had ever even dreamt of the establishment of the Indian Military Force.

Four persons including Dal Singh were deputed for recruitment, and each of whom were required to recruit at least seven patriots, whose names were to be given to the German Camp Commander and while enlisting them, who would keep in mind that these recruits must be hostile to the British. Twenty-eight prisoners were selected and they were sent to Kuniesberg for further assimilation with the Military Force. This was a top secret mission, which continued even after the departure of Netaji. Dal Singh and Sardar Sohan Singh met Netaji thrice in Berlin and submitted their written reports. All plans were prepared in accordance with military discipline. Three battalions were raised and all of which had German officers as Commanders and Company Commanders.

India Brigade was armed with hand-held weapons like machine guns, mortars, rifles, anti-tank guns, grenades and revolvers. This brigade guarded with the German Army, who guarded the coastal border. But, when the British forces entered Normandy and started advancing, they were confronted with the Indian Military Force and a fight ensued. The Indian Military Force had to suffer great loss and ultimately they had to surrender near Bonn and the remainder of the force were made prisoners. All these prisoners were taken to Italy, from where they were sent to Toronto port and then back to Bombay. From Bombay, these prisoners were sent to Asodha Camp in Rohtak district, where they were tried for treason. During enquiry, they were divided into three groups - grey, red and white. Those who joined the Indian Military Force, were neither given a pension nor paid for the period they spent in jail.

German officers, who were associated with the Indian prisoners' camp, were eager to learn Hindi. Prisoners also wanted to learn Hindi. As such, the Camp Commander was contacted and within a week, all essential items like blackboards, exercise books, inkpots, pencils etc., were provided and Hindi classes started. Two sections were created. Dal Singh and Bhim Singh Ajmeri took the teaching responsibility. Similarly, German was taught in these classes. These classes continued regularly from 1940 to 1943 and during this period, about 1,000 prisoners learnt Hindi.

❑

7.

When Hitler started using the Indian Military Force arbitrarily, Netaji expressed his desire to go to Japan. Hitler called his Naval Officers and asked their views in this regard. They told him that the task was highly risky and there was just 25 per cent chance of survival, as the allied navies were very strong and Japan's submarines would have to cross their path. Netaji was told about the risks involved in his journey to Japan.

Netaji said, "I will go, even if the chance of survival is one percent."

Netaji started his journey in a Japanese submarine and he was accompanied by Kanwal Singh, a jawan of the Indian Military Force, and others as his bodyguards. Kanwal Singh was an expert swimmer. Besides him, Aabid Khan was also with Netaji. This journey by submarines was fraught with risks and was awful. The British government had laid mines on its sea routes. In addition to this, it had also devices at various places, which could detect submarine passing that way. But, the German submarine, Netaji was travelling in, was fitted with the latest lethal weapons. During this journey, one day the crew spotted a British vessel. The Military Officer of the German submarine tried to torpedo the ship, but due to carelessness, the submarine surfaced. As soon as the submarine was sighted, the enemy ship decided to destroy it. The German Captain ordered the crew to take a dive to save the submarine from the enemy's assault, but the submerging process took a little more. In the meantime, the enemy ship pushed it violently, which made the submarine tilt, but it however, survived. This journey took three months to complete. Netaji reached Sumatra Island on 6th May. He was received at the port by several Japanese Officers. Colonel Satoshi Yamamoto immediately recognized Netaji. Colonel Satoshi Yamamoto had been in Berlin as the Military Attaché and both of them had become intimate friends in Germany. Subhas Chandra Bose had to stay at Sabang port for five days. Thereafter, he was flown to Japan. It was a hopping flight and on his way, Subhas Chandra Bose stayed one day each at Penang, Saigon, Manila and Taipei. On May 16, 1943, he reached the grand city of Tokyo, where many people were eagerly waiting for him and where future history was in the making. In Germany, Netaji was conferred the title of 'His Excellency Majotta'. During his journey in the submarine, he was code-named 'Mastuda' and he was to be addressed as Subhas Bose in Japan. From Tokyo, he took a flight for Singapore, where Yalappa Dr. Lakshmi, Shahnawaz Khan and other leaders were anxiously waiting for him at the airport. Indian and Japanese Military Officers were also attentively waiting for Subhas Babu. With a screeching sound, the plane touched the tarmac. As the plane came to a halt, all emotionally-charged leaders and military officers rushed to receive him.

All eyes were riveted on Subhas Babu. Alighting from the plane, Subhas Babu looked like an angel. He was moved by the pleasure and eagerness of the people.[4]

Addressing them, he said, "Brothers! I feel elated finding myself amongst you. We have to liberate our motherland and write a new history."

Captain Ram Singh started playing a melodious tune on his violin and Miss Saraswati animatedly began a song:

"Subhasji, the spirit of Hind has arrived. Subhasji, the pride of Hind has arrived."

Netaji, Rash Babu, Aabir Hassan, Japanese soldiers and others were present at the airport. A reporter asked Netaji, "What kind of administration system would you prefer in the India of tomorrow?"

Netaji replied, "What rights Britain, who is considered to be the father of democracy, have over India, where 20 per cent of the world's humanity lives, to trample its people, to devoid them of their rights, to destroy their culture and to rule them? How can they claim themselves to be the protector of democracy? Yet, they present themselves as the supporter of democracy on the basis of a false and artificial judicial system.

Later, Rash Behari Bose casually told Netaji, "Subhas Babu, I am tired now. Please handle all the sources from now onwards."

"Don't say it again."

"No, Subhas! I am really tired."

"Rash Babu, I have to learn a lot from revolutionaries like you. You have to guide me, kindly don't dishearten and disappoint me with such talks."[5]

And then, Rash Behari Bose appointed Netaji as the Commander of the Indian National Army (Azad Hind Fauz). Immediately after taking over as the Commander of Indian

National Army (INA), Netaji called upon Indians to enlist for the INA to fight for liberation of the country.

Thousands of young men and women started heading for Singapore for recruitment in the INA. I had gone to the nearby Sankrod village to see the Teej fair. This fair might still be organized at the shore of Yamuna. It used to be held in those days. My mother used to give one rupee for the fair and even after spending money on eateries and purchasing various articles, we used to save a lot of paise. We used to go to the festival in a bullock cart during those days, but later 'jhotha buggies' had been introduced and people used to ride in those buggies for the Teej fair.

There was still time for returning home from the fair, I was informed by my friend and sworn sister-in-law, Phullo Devi's husband, Ram Singh, son of Shri Chhajju Singh[6], who was my godfather's namesake, who had come home on leave, that he was influenced by Netaji's appeal to join the freedom struggle. This time he would not go back to the service of the British Empire, but would be leaving for Singapore to join Netaji. I had asked him, "Brother, who are the others accompanying you to Singapore?"

"A number of Jat boys are coming with me."

"Who are they?"

"They include your second sworn brother Sardar Singh Toofan, Ratan Singh son of Kanak Singh of Sarurupur, Ram Lal son of Nathu of Ghitaura, Umrao Singh of Sumhera, Murari Arya[7] of Fakharpur, Karan Singh Tomar of Bawali, and Sirdare, Lahari Singh, Girwar Singh, Kalu, Begraj, Anoop, Zile Singh, Alam Singh, Khacheru, Bhim, Nadan and Mahavir Singh of Dhikoli."

"Please take me also with you to Singapore, I have come to know that girls are also coming forward to join the INA."

"But you are the daughter of a bania, how could you fire a gun? Instead of a gun, taraju (a scale) adorns your hands."

"Brother, pan of the scale would be shield for me and the tongue of the scale would not be less than a gun for me."

Instantly, another sworn brother from Sanklod, Sardar Singh also arrived there, who was a lyricist and wrote folk songs under the pen-name of 'Toofan'. He said, "Listen, sister, I have written a beautiful ragini on Subhas Chandra Bose today, which lists articles, which she wants her brother-in-law to bring from his return from a foreign country..it describes all this.."

"What had she demanded?" With these words I took the slip from him and after going through it, I said, "I'll sing this ragini, I'll set the tune myself, as I am a trained musician."

"Very good!" said the folk musician and a soldier, Ram Singh brought an earthen pitcher and after fixing a piece of rubber tube on its mouth started playing it and Sardar Singh Toofan also started clapping his hands rhythmically. I started singing the ragini, gist of which was as follows:

Bos isee sari lyaade ho, jiskee chamak niraalee
Bos isee sari lyaade ho, jiskee chamak niraalee
Sari upar photu kema, bhaarat ke sabhee arya hon
Tilak Gokhle Rishi Dayanand Swami shankrachary hon
Gauramint jhan us dillee mai Rajagopalacharya hon
Rakshamantree Bharat ke Baladev Singh Sardar bhi hon
Rajendraprasad Patel Gandhi Veer Jawahar bhi hon
Hanste-hanste jelon andar padane ko taiyaar bhi hon
Kaale paanee pahunchae jinhonne jaan khapaalee
Bos isee sari lyaade ho, jisakee chamak niraalee

Chandrsekhar Veer Bhagat Singh Rasbihari Bos bhi hon
Lala Lajapataray Lahor mai pitate hue nirdosh bhi hon
Rajguru Sukhadev v Bismil marate hue mai josh bhi ho
Jaliyanvaale Baag ka jalasa, Dayar phaayar karata ho
Bhaarat ka badala lene landan mai sher bicharata ho
Udham singh ki goli sai landan mai Daayar marata ho
Daayar mara aap mara gaya na vaar kati khaallee
Bos isee sari lyaade ho, jisakee chamak niraalee

Ram aur Lakshman rajchodke banme dhakke khate hon
Harishchandr bhi sty ke karan kashi mai bik jaate hon
Jagdepawar katkai gardan dan mai shish chadhate hon?
Mordhvaj bhi chir kai ladaka Karsan ka sher jimate hon
Hirnakush Prahalaad bhakt ko lal khambh pakdate hon
Raja Bhoj bikramaadity praja ka kasht mitaate hon
Din aajaadee ka ho, milake sab poojai deevaalee
Bos isee sari lyaade ho, jisakee chamak niraalee

Ramayan Mahabharat Geeta dhaarmik itihaas bhi ho
Azaadee aatee dikhai aur gulaamee ka naash bhee ho
Lalkilepai Tirangajhanda samne khada Subhas bhi ho
SardarsinghTufan kah guru Prthvisingh umang mai hon
Majdur kisano ka sevak Sar Choturam bhi sang mai hon
Bhaaratma ka bachcha bachcha azadi ki jang mein hon
Sankarod ke nakshe mein sab dikhain haalee-paalee
Bos isee sari lyaade ho, jisakee chamak niraalee[8]

"O! Bose bring for me a lustrous sari, a sari with excellent lustre, which has photos of all the Aryas of India, Tilak, Gokhale, Rishi Dayanand Swami, Shankaracharya, there should be the government in Delhi, which should also have Rajagopalachari, Sardar Baldev Singh as Defence Minister, Rajendra Prasad, Patel, Gandhi and Brave Jawahar, who are prepared to go to jail with a smile, who readily wasted their lives in penal servitude in Andamans, get me a lustrous sari with excellent....

The sari should also have the photos of Chandrashekhar, Vir Bhagat Singh, Rash Behari Bose and also Lala Lajpat Rai and of innocents beaten at Lahore and also the passion of Rajguru, Sudhdev and Bismil facing death, also the festive crowd at Jalianwala Bagh, also Dyer firing on the crowd, and Udham Singh, the lion roaming on the London streets and dying Dyer with the bullets of Udham Singh, Dyer died; not a mark was missed by Udham Singh. O Bose, bring a sari for me, which has a unique shine.

Relinquishing the throne, Ram and Lakshaman lived a hard life in the forest; for the sake of truth Harishchandra sells himself at Kashi; Jagdev Panwar, who beheads himself and offer it as donation; King Mordhwaj, who kills his son and offer it to the lion of Lord Krishna for food; Hirnakush made his son a devotee of god, to embrace the red hot pole; King Bhoj Vikramaditya removed the sufferings of his subjects. It should be the day of freedom, when all celebrate Diwali. O Bose, bring a sari for me, which has a unique shine.

There should be the Ramayana, the Mahabharata, the Gita and all religious history on it; freedom is seen nearing and slavery meets its end; the tricolour is hoisted at the Red Fort, facing which should be attentive Subhas; Sardar Singh Toofan says, there should also be ecstatic Guru Prithavi Singh, servants of workers and farmers, Chhotu Ram. Even the children of Mother India participate in this war for freedom. All should appear happy and healthy on this map of Sankrod. O Bose, bring a sari for me, which has a unique shine."

After singing this ragini, I once again forcefully requested them and finally they agreed to include me in their team, which was leaving for Singapore to join the INA. Thus, I reached Singapore.

In fact, all those who were joining the INA, were British Army fugitives and they wanted to get rid of the guilt, they were carrying, of serving the British Army as such they had chosen the path of making a sacrifice for liberating their motherland.

During 1942, when the British atrocities were at their extreme, all of them had left the service of the British. Even warrants had been issued against some of these persons.

After independence, for his service in the INA, Sardar Singh Toofan was appointed as a singer in All India Radio and he had sung this ragini in his melodious voice over All India Radio several times.[9] I listen to this ragini even today, but the singers have changed.

❑

8.

Netaji was to be felicitated at the Padang ground in Singapore. Attired like a soldier, Netaji travelled in a car. He had Rash Behari Bose and Colonel Bhonsale with him. A convoy of 10-12 motor cycles was leading his car and was followed by a few army vehicles. He was wearing a well-stitched Khaki military shirt and a military cap with two buttons. He wore knee-length leather boots and a fitting khaki pant, which reached his knee. On the right side of his coat, he was wearing medals and one of which had the tricolour imprinted and the other had the map of united India. Along with soldiers, civilians had gathered in large numbers to see and hear him.

Looking at the huge gathering, Netaji asked, "How many of you are willing to sacrifice your life in protecting Mother India? Tell me."

In response to the call by Netaji, soldiers raised their rifles. All of them stood up and the air ranted with the slogans of Chalo Delhi, Chalo Delhi. Netaji was filled with pride. In a choked voice he said, "My brave brothers! Today, I announce to the world with pleasure and pride, behold our freedom fighter army is ready for liberating India from foreign yoke. Brothers, history is the best teacher. I have learnt from Swami Dayanand Saraswati that dynasties that rise, also fall. Standing on this British graveyard in Singapore, I say that the tale of British supremacy has come to an end and has been buried in history."

Netaji also raised a platoon of women, which was named Rani Lakshmi Bai Regiment. Dr. Lakshmi was the commander of the Regiment and my friend Manvati Arya was appointed secretary. I was enlisted in the Lakshmi Bai Regiment and Netaji was impressed by my abilities and soon, I turned into his confidant. Netaji addressed another public meeting at the ground of Kuala Lumpur. Addressing a gathering of about three thousand, Netaji said, "Mothers and sisters, show to the world, that women with their deeds, can transform themselves into lightning, which is capable of shaking the heaven. Women like Chandbibi, Ahilyabai, Maharani Padmini, Rani of Jhansi have created the glorious history of India. I invite all of you to join the Indian National Army."

After the inspiring speech of Netaji, there was non-stop influx of generous donors for the cause of INA. There was a photographer girl, who donated his ear-rings to Netaji and got herself enlisted in the INA. Similarly, many persons gave all their wealth for the country and joined the INA, ready to sacrifice their lives for the liberation of Mother India.

Ultimately, on October 21, 1943, Subhas Chandra Bose announced in Singapore the establishment of an interim government. Various governments including those of Japan, Germany, Italy, China, etc., gave recognition to the independent entity of the Indian National Government. This government issued its own currency.

❑

9.

Pavitra Mohan Roy was the chief of the Intelligence Department of the Indian National Army, which controlled both the male and female intelligence wings, but I had the honour of becoming the first lady spy of the Indian National Army. I was bestowed with this responsibility by Netaji Subhas Chandra Bose himself. Along with colleagues, Manvati Arya and Durga Malla Gorkha and Daniel Cowley, I left no stone unturned in spying for Netaji against the British. There was another girl, Saraswati Rajmani also with me. She was younger to me and was a Burmese-origin citizen of Burma. Both of us were entrusted the task of spying on the British officers. We got ourselves dressed up like boys and started working at British officers' houses and military camps. We gathered sufficient information for the INA. We had to keep our ears open, discuss the gathered information with our colleagues, and then send it to Netaji. Occasionally, we used to lay our hands on important documents. When all of us girls were being deputed on the espionage tasks, we were clearly told to shoot ourselves, in the event of being caught by the enemy. A girl failed to follow this instruction and was caught alive. It put all the colleagues and the organization into danger.

Rajmani and I decided to extricate her from the enemy's clutches. We dressed like eunuchs and reached the place where our colleague Durga was being kept as a prisoner. We drugged the officers and fled from the place along with Durga. But while fleeing, we met with an accident. The guard fired from his rifle which hit Rajmani's right leg and she started bleeding profusely. Somehow, along with myself and Durga,

limping Rajmani also managed to climb a large tree. The search operation continued underneath and we had to remain hiding on that tree for three long days without food and water. After three days, we mustered courage and safely returned to the INA base. The bullet lodged in her leg, made Rajmani limp for the rest of her life. Netaji was pleased about Rajmani's courageous act and she was promoted to the rank of lieutenant in the INA. Rajmani and I were appointed bodyguards to Netaji.

❑

10.

Netaji loved to remain among soldiers. Finding Netaji in their midst, soldiers were reminded of the era of Lord Rama. It was for the first time, when the supreme leader of India was himself leading the war for freedom. That night, Netaji had discussions with his officers late into the night and then he retired to his camp. That day, responsibility for the protection of the camp was on Rani Lakshmi Bai Regiment. I was also deployed as a guard to Netaji. I was at the back of the tent. With rifle in hand, I was attentively guarding the tent. It was about 2 am. All the soldiers were fast asleep having sweet dreams of independent India. Many sentries too were lying here and there in their deep slumber, but as a soldier, I was doing my duty diligently. It was a dark night of the last day of the dark half of the month. The wind was whistling. It was a pitch dark night. Amidst horrifying lull and wails of a cat, my ears were tuned to hear foot-falls and the slightest of sound and my eyes were trained to see like a bat. At that moment, I felt as if someone was lying in ambush near me and felt something nasty was going to happen...but I was sure that I was not mistaken...somebody was definitely there...

"Stop" when I saw a shadow approaching, I shouted, "stop there and reveal your code."

"I am a spy, I have very important information for Netaji," the shadow said.

The voice appeared familiar to me, but when the shadow came near me, I screamed, "Srikant, you!"

"Yes, I am Srikant", he said, "I have come here to kill Netaji."

"Listen, I implore you to go back, otherwise...."

"You can't do anything," Srikant said, "because you are an Indian woman and an Indian woman can neither arrest nor kill her husband."

"Look, I warn you, if you move a step further, you are in for big trouble."

"And if I do not kill Netaji, I'll not only lose my job, but will also be imprisoned."

"Why don't you join the INA, it would be the best service in the world."

"The best job in the world!" Tauntingly Srikant had said, "should I go to Kalapani for conniving with the traitors against the British?"

"Kalapani is not less than a pilgrimage."

"Just shut up and let me finish my task," saying this, Srikant Jayranjan Das tried to enter Netaji's tent and fired to kill Netaji, but bullets hit Col. Nizamuddin, the driver of Netaji. Meanwhile, I pushed my rifle into the side of my husband saying, "O God! Forgive this husband killer."[10]

But Srikant was alert. Gathering himself up, he fired two shots with his revolver at me. He had tried to kill me, but I was fortunate enough as the bullets missed my forehead, as one pierced my ear and the other just kissed my neck. Blood started oozing out and shouting

'Jai Hind', I fell unconscious, bracing myself for my eternal journey…a new journey, and fell on ground like an uprooted tree falling in the abyss. I didn't know what happened to Srikant or what he did..

❑

11.

What is death? What does it look like? We had read about death being a beautiful thing in the tales. Death is a beloved, with whom a person meets one day or the other. However hard we wish, we can't evade it. Death brings with it the end to all your sorrows. Death liberates you from this body of yours and takes you to a new beginning. Who had said such things, when these had been said and why had been said, I don't remember, but it appears from my experience that death is really a beautiful happening.

Hit by two bullets, when I fell down, my heart began to beat very fast, as if it was racing, and racing it was, against death. I was feeling dizzy. I was feeling as if there had been two holes in my head and I was on the verge of death. This was the time, when I was going to die and I had been looking at my death, which appeared at hand. This is the time, when the body is expected to communicate with the mind about the impending death, which is about to be engulfed by a void, in a moment. The mind, then realizes that it is in serious trouble and, it is only who, that can rescue itself from the trouble.

I was dying, and nobody was listening to me. Suddenly, I felt as if I was surrounded by colours. I was visualizing strange scenes in my mind. And, this was the journey that I undertook after my death or during my unconsciousness after being hit by the bullets. I had left my body. At first, I saw wet clouds. Then I saw something which resembled the view of space being seen from a telescope. Different colours were merging with each other. There was silence all around. All this was happening around me and I was only feeling it. All this was very beautiful to me. I felt, as if I was being pulled out by somebody above. I felt as if my whole body had turned into a lung. Suddenly my entire body disappeared. And then I felt as if I was in space. Suddenly, I saw a bright light. It was a grand blue light, as if the entire light of the world had focused there, I felt as if someone was pulling me. I was trying to look at myself, but I was not there. There was not a trace of darkness, there was light all around, but I was unable to see my shadow there. If a person is in light, then he is able to see his or her shadow, but there was no shadow of mine. That was the moment, when I was startled. But I was not afraid. I was looking at the light, the whole and grand light, but I was unable to see myself. But the only feeling that I had, was of eternal peace, love, energy and beauty...as if I was the eyes only...I didn't remember whether I had a body or not...still I didn't feel loneliness or solitude. I was feeling others who were there, but was unable to see them. But they were there, because they were able to communicate with me. I was being welcomed there. But, then all of a sudden all this stopped. As if all of this had merged with one another. Everything appeared to have merged with that supernatural light and turned into one...everything had turned into a void.

The last thing that I remember was that suddenly I had been pushed. That was startling, but I was happy. And then, perhaps I had been bidden farewell. On the earth, my dead heart had suddenly started beating again, as Netaji had called an ambulance and I was immediately shifted to an interim military hospital, but he was aghast. Doctors told him that she had been brought to the hospital late. She had been dead for the last 15 to 45 minutes. But Netaji was adamant and said, "Please, save this brave soldier. The country needs her." And at that very moment, I started breathing again. I have shared the experience of my journey of 15 and 45 minutes with you. Those had been my valuable moments, which only I had lived in. When I regained consciousness, Netaji told me, "Before the wounded Srikant could enter my tent, I woke up and other sentries had also reached there."

❑

12.

"Arrest him." Netaji ordered his security personnel and as he placed his hand on my forehead, tears oozed out of his eyes, "Sister, you have paid the debt to the Motherland by becoming Nagini. When we reach Delhi, we will inscribe your name and name of your Khekda village at the top of the martyrs memorial at the Red Fort. Jai Hind!"

"You are great, Amma! You have served in Netaji's Indian National Army!" I was amazed, but she said calmly, "No..no, Netaji was not the founder of the INA, as I have already told you."

"Then, who initially founded it?" I asked her.

"It was Raja Mahendra Pratap, who with the help of Germany, and in coordination with Harishchandra, son of Swami Shraddhanand established the Indian National Army. I don't remember the date, but it was during December 1915 and it was Raja Mahendra Pratap's birthday, he had turned 28. He established the first Indian government-in-exile. Later, after 28 years, Subhas Chandra Bose had similarly constituted the Azad Hind Government in Singapore. Raja Mahendra Pratap was appointed head of the state, i.e. first President of Azad

Hind Government and Maulavi Barkatullah was declared the Prime Minister and Obeduallah Sindhi as the Home Minister.

"Later Barkatuallah University was established which was named after Maulavi Barkatullah of Bhopal. This Kabul government of the Raja formally declared war against the British. The Raja Government appointed its ambassadors almost to every country and they started efforts for getting recognition of the concerned government. But, in those days, neither was there any effective military strategy nor did they have any Bose-like support for this revolutionary idea. But, Raja's fight did not end here. His life was full of chaos. He was the real Arya Peshwa."[11]

"It is interesting to note that the year during which Raja established his first government-in-exile, also saw the return of Gandhiji from South Africa, who was encouraging the Indian youth to join the British Army and he was even named the enlisting sergeant for the British Army. The British government had announced bounty on the head of Raja, it had seized his state Mursan and declared Raja as a fugitive. Raja had suffered for a long time during his life. Then, he went to Japan, where he started a magazine titled *World Federation*. For quite a long time, he continued to reveal to the world the atrocities of the British Government. During the Second World War, Raja set up an executive board to force the British to leave India. But, by the end of the war, the British Government's attitude towards Raja had turned soft. Then, the independence of India had also become almost a realty. Raja was allowed to return to India. After 32 years, Raja returned to India and he landed at Madras coast in 1946. From there, he did not go to his house, but went straight to Wardha to meet Gandhiji. Anyway, Gandhi's non-violence ruined the country....Gandhiji was against armed revolution.

Once, Subhas met Vitthalbhai Patel in Europe and both of them had a long discussion, which was referred to as 'Patel-Bose Analysis'. Both of them had condemned the leadership of Gandhi in this analysis. Later, when Vitthalbhai Patel fell ill, Subhas nursed him for quite a long time. But Vitthalbhai could not be saved. He died. In his will, Vitthalbhai Patel bequeathed his entire property to Subhas, so that it could be used for his armed revolution. But after his death, his younger brother Sardar Vallabh Bhai Patel refused to recognize this will on the advice of Gandhiji. Sardar Patel took this will to the court. After winning this case, Sardar Patel donated his entire property to the cause of Gandhi's harijan welfare mission. Had this been used for the armed revolution, the country would have been freed long back..." Saying all this, Amma had become sentimental...I offered her some juice, after taking it she again asked for going to the toilet, both of us took her to the washroom, but within no time she requested us to take her back to her bed. After a while, she resumed her story, "in 1942 an army was raised, you may call it either Azad Hind Fauj or Indian National Army." Then she stopped talking about Raja Mahendra Pratap Singh and concentrated on her Azad Hind, "an Indian, Ras Behari Bose, who was residing in Tokyo (Japan), called a conference on March 28–30, 1942 for deliberating on the issue of raising the Indian National Army (Azad Hind Fauj). The INA was formed with the active co-operation of Captain Mohan Singh, Ras Behari Bose and Niranjan Singh Gill. Initially, the INA was the idea of Mohan Singh. Meanwhile, the Indian Independence League was formed for Indians living abroad, the first conference of which was organized in June 1942 at Bangkok. The first division of the INA was formed on December 1, 1942 under Mohan Singh."

"Amma, from where did they got so many soldiers?" I couldn't stop asking.

"They had grown a tree of men!"

"What do you mean?"

"O my innocent daughter!" She said, "Where do you think, man would have come, they were their own men...Among those fortunate persons, about 16,300 were soldiers. In fact, Japan had released 60,000 war prisoners for recruitment to the Indian National Army. But in view of the dispute between the Japan government and soldiers under Mohan Singh about the role of the INA, Mohan Singh and Niranjan Singh Gill were arrested."

"What happened next?"

"What was there to happen?" Amma said, "The second phase of the Indian National Army began only when Netaji went to Singapore. Netaji, however, had already formed the Indian Military Group (Indian League) in 1941 at Berlin, but when Germany tried to use this Group for their own ends, problems cropped up and Bose decided to head for South East Asia. Netaji Subhas Chandra Bose reached Singapore, which was under Japanese control, in July 1943 travelling by a German submarine. There, he gave the famous slogan "Delhi Chalo" (March to Delhi). On July 4, 1943, Subhas Chandra Bose took control of the Indian National Army and Indian League. An interim Government of India as the Azad Hind Government was formed at Singapore on October 21, 1943. Germany, Japan and their allied countries gave recognition to the Azad Hind Government. Then, Netaji made Singapore and Rangoon as the headquarters of the Indian National Army. Addressing Gandhiji on Radio in July 1944, Subhas Chandra Bose said, "The final war for the freedom of India has begun.

O, Father of the Nation, we seek your blessings and good wishes in this sacred war." Besides, brigades of the Army were also named after Indian leaders - Mahatma Gandhi Brigade, Abdul Kalam Azad Brigade, Jawaharlal Nehru Brigade and Subhas Chandra Bose Brigade. Shah Nawaz Khan was the commander of the Subhas Chandra Brigade. And mine was Rani Jhasi Brigade..as you know..

"Subhas Chandra Bose was addressing a meeting on July 12, 1943 at Singapore, which was attended by about 25,000 women from various countries. During that meeting formation of a Women's Regiment was announced and 20 women soldiers were recruited on July 15, 1943 for that regiment. By the end of the month, 50 women soldiers had been recruited for the Rani Jhansi Regiment. Dr. Lakshmi Swaminathan was appointed first Captain of the regiment. Thereafter, during August 1943, 500 women were selected for military training. Out of which only 150 woman soldiers were selected for the Rani Jhansi Regiment. On October 22, 1943, Netaji announced the formation of the Rani Jhansi regiment. By then, 1,000 women had been recruited for this regiment.

"This regiment was peculiar in a way, as all of its women soldiers were called rani. After Singapore, a second training camp was established at Tiganue in Rangoon. The Thiver sisters, Navratnam sisters, Rojamma, Arya and Blance Thivi were the chief naiks of the Regiment. This regiment was divided into two departments: Military and Familiarity. Soldiers were allowed to join the regiment only after intense training. All women soldiers were asked to wear khaki uniforms and had to wear their hair short. Rank badges were pinned on shoulder flaps.

A middle-aged Amma turned up at the Rani Jhansi Regiment for recruitment, but for reasons of health, she was not recruited. I had come from Lucknow and was teaching at the Montessori School at Cantt. Road (Nazirabad). She said that her revolutionary husband had died during the testing of a bomb. When she insisted on joining the Regiment, Netaji put her on the task of making button-holes and putting buttons on soldiers' uniforms. Her name was Durga, whom I used to call Durga Bhabhi out of affection. There was another soldier in the INA, whose name too was Durga or Durga Mall, who was later promoted as Major by Netaji and he was collecting intelligence for the Intelligence Department like me.

One day, Durga Mall came to Durga Bhabhi for getting a button stitched to his shirt and looking at her, he said, "Durgaji, you are not Bhabhi, but you are Mother India!"

"Go away, you fool," smilingly Durga Bhabhi had said.

"No, I am telling the truth."

"All right, if you are telling me the truth, then what can you do for me?"

"When I have recognized you as Mother India, then what is there to be done? I have to sacrifice everything for Mother India, and I have also been blessed by you. The buttons you have stitched on our uniforms are no less than the Sudarshan Chakra (circular weapon of Lord Vishnu) or shield for us. O Bhabhi, if the enemy is not a coward and fire at the chest instead of the back, then the bullet would rebound after hitting the button and kill the poor enemy."

"And if the bullet misses the button and pierces the heart, then?" Durga had aksed.

"How can it pierce the heart, as before that I would blow the head of the enemy with my bullet."

"Even then?"

"Then these buttons would act like Veer Chakra on my dead body and make me honoured'." After a while he said, "look mother Bhabi, whenever these brave hearts are decorated with medals in independent India, I am confident that the word *chakra* will be added to the medals, as you have started the tradition of these medals, by putting them on the alive martyrs."

"You are crazy, why are you talking of living martyrs, just think of flying the Azad Hind flag at the Red fort, after defeating enemies."

When the Army was ready to march for the war, Netaji had convinced Durga Bhabhi to leave for Lucknow. "Mother, you'll have to go, just see, I married in Germany, i.e. I sought help from Hitler and gathered Indians from all over the world to form this marriage procession and I am coming to Delhi with the Indian National Army. I want you to conduct the *Aarati* ceremony for not only the bride and the bridegroom but also for this entire marriage procession at the Red Fort, when we get there."

"Subhas Babu, please accept this *neg* (present given at the time of marriage)," saying this, she put her small bundle before him, which she had kept secure till then. Netaji opened the bundle, which contained several kilos of silver ornaments and a *hansuli* of gold (ornamental collar).

Netaji said, "Mother, I can't accept this gift from a helpless lady."

"Then deposit the money, which you get in lieu of these, in the INA Bank, return it to me when the country gets independence. I can't deposit these in any British Bank, as the British themselves are plunderers. One must keep one's money in one's bank only....if this money is used for the country, then only will the country prosper," Durga had said.

"All right," accepting the ornaments, Netaji gave a written document to her saying that Durga Bhabhi had donated her entire money as an aid to the INA and the moment the country achieves independence, she would be given a pension for her entire life.

Later, while leaving for Lucknow, Durga Bhabhi handed over the receipt to me and said, "Keep it safe, Beti, it will help you. You have your whole life before you. and this is what I can offer to my god-daughter...you have sacrificed your *suhag* (auspicious wifehood) for the country."

"You too have sacrificed your *suhag*, Amma, brother Bhagwati Charan Bohra too.." I had paused as I had become so sentimental that it was not possible for me to utter a word.

❑

13.

"Subhas Chandra Bose had called upon the soldiers, "You give me blood, I'll give you independence."

"Subhas Chandra Bose was President, Prime Minister and also the Chief of the Army Staff. The Finance Department was entrusted to S.C. Chatterjee, whereas S.A. Aiyar was made in-charge of the publicity wing and Lakshmi Swaminathan was made responsible for the Women's Organization."

"And, what task was entrusted to you, Amma..."

"Me..." She said, "Intelligence Department and...."

With a sigh, she kept silent, I asked her, "Enough, now Amma you should rest, we'll talk about it later."

"Daughter!" She said, "If I don't tell you my story, then one page of history will remain blank. Nobody will be able to know about it, not even the researchers would be enlightened, as after the defeat, Netaji had himself destroyed all the records, so that we are not made to suffer."

Japan gifted Andaman and Nicobar islands to Netaji for his Government. Subhas visited these islands and gave new names to them. Andaman was called Shahid Dweep (Martyr Island)

and Nicobar as Swaraj Dweep (Own-rule Island). He hoisted the flag of independent India on these islands on December 30, 1943. After hoisting the tricolour at gymkhana ground (now known as Netaji Stadium), Netaji addressed revolutionaries, soldiers of the Indian National Army and public and said that the story of India's independence that started at Andaman, would end by hoisting the flag at the Viceroy House in Delhi. Government of India has built a memorial at the Gymkhana Ground in Port Blair, where Netaji had hoisted the tricolour. The Andaman administration organizes various programmes on 30th December every year. The emblem of the Indian National Army had a roaring tiger on its flag.

"Our organization had martial song, which we the soldiers used to hum, which filled us with new enthusiasm. The gist of the marching song is as follows:

Kadam kadam badhae ja
khushee ke geet gaaye ja
ye jindagee hai kaum kee
too kaum pe lutaaye ja

too sher-e-hind aage badh
marane se too kabhee na dar
uda ke dushmanon ka sar
josh-e-vatan badhaaye ja

himmat teree badhatee rahe
khuda teree sunata rahe
jo saamane tere khade
too khaak mein milaaye ja

chalo dillee pukaar ke
kaumee-nishaan sambhaal ke
laal kile pe gaad ke
laharaaye ja laharaaye jaaee12

"March O Soldier march, and sing the songs of happiness. This life has been given to you by the nation and you should sacrifice it for the nation. March forward you, Lions of India, with no fear of death. Kill the enemies and keep the nation's morale high. May you be more and more courageous. May God listen to you. Whosoever dares to confront you, bring him to his death. March to Delhi, keeping the national flag high and pitch it at the Red Fort and fly it, fly it."

"The Indian National Army attacked the British again on February 4, 1944. It was a terrible attack. The INA along with Japanese troops reached the Indian plains of Kohima and Imphal on March 18, 1944, traversing a long route via Rangoon (Yagoon). Some Indian regions including Kohima, Palel etc., were freed from the British. My colleague in the Intelligence Department, Daniel Cawley played an important role in this successful campaign, as he had collected and provided all important information on spying on the border, especially about entering India."

"Amma, then why was the INA defeated? Was it due to the lack of support from Gandhji or Nehruji?"

"Gandhiji used to say, if one slaps you on one cheek, offer him another cheek...but the British! The British had slapped all of us so hard that our cheeks were swollen, that was the reason that even Gandhiji had to call people to do or die... similar to the incident in the Mahabharat, when Lord Krishna, who had vowed not to take to arms during the war against the Kauravas, was made to take up arms by Bhishma Pitamah. Netaji had a great regard for Gandhiji, but he was forced to take to the path of revolution and to constitute an Army, as no ruler can cede its empire just for the fear of truth and non-violence? Since the creation of this world, there has been not

a single example of relinquishing the rule of a country by a cruel despot to somebody else."

"You are going astray, Amma....I had asked you, why your army lost? What were the reasons for the defeat?"

"Our own people defeated us....had Gandhji and Nehruji stood by us..." then she abruptly stopped and then she said, "brigades of the INA fought along with the Japanese at India's eastern border and Burma, but unfortunately, with the defeat of Japanese forces in the Second World War, the INA had also to face the defeat."

"How?"

The 14th British regiment had captured Burma during the Second World War in 1943, defeating the Japanese Army. With this victory, the war report sent by reporters who had accompanied the British Army, made most of the people aware of the heroic deeds of the INA. That is why the censorship was imposed on the activities of the INA by the British, came to light. Despite this, the British Intelligence set-up decided to tarnish the image of the INA. British Viceroy Wavell had always described the INA as a group of cowards and weak persons.

Durga Bhabhi had left, but Durga Bhaiya was at the front.

Brother Durga Mall was arrested by the enemy forces on March 27, 1944 in Ukhrul near Kohima in Manipur, while he tried to gather important information.

After being made war-prisoner and his trial, he was subjected to fearsome torture. He was brought to the central jail in the Red Fort on August 15, 1944 and the farce of trial continued for nine days, and he was sentenced to death. In fact, these nine days were the auspicious *navratri* days for Durga Mall....

Before sentencing him to death, he was offered some lighter sentence instead of death sentence, if he acknowledged the crime of sedation and revealed all the secrets about Netaji. To put psychological pressure and make him sentimental, Durga Bhaiya was made to meet his wife Sharda, but Major Durga told her, 'my sacrifice won't go waste. I am confident that India will attain its independence. Just for a few more days, Sharda, don't worry, crores of Indians are with you.' Sharda went back to her native place of Dharmshala in Himachal Pradesh. Durga Mall had spent just three days with his wife after his marriage.

One shudders to imagine the severe circumstances, when one realizes that these words were spoken to his wife by a person, who had spent just three days after the marriage with his wife and was meeting her after three years and that too under the shadow of death...

My brother, Major Durga Mall had neither given up to pressure nor acknowledged working for the INA as an act of sedation. He was sentenced to death on 15th August and the sunrise of August 25, 1944 came as the sunset for his life. But, when there is darkness, a ray of light appears, and I could not forget the contribution of Durga Mall to the independence of the country...

"Then, what happened?"

"Something inevitable," she continued, "Soldiers and officers of the Indian National Army were arrested by the British in 1945."

"What about you?"

"I was also arrested, but after a few seconds of hearing before a magistrate, I was taken to an unknown place, whereas the brave soldiers and officers, who had fought for liberating the country, were tried for treason at the Red Fort in Delhi during November 1945. Col. Sehgal, Col. Dhillon and Major Shahnawaz Khan were the main accused in this trial, who were accused of treason. In the beginning, no one came in support of them, even Nehruji had kept his distance from these warriors, but after realizing public sentiments, who had taken to the street, Sir Tej Bahadur Sapru, Jawaharlal Nehru, Bhula Bhai Desai and K.N. Katju argued for them in the court. But, the court, however, sentenced these people to death. The ruling was condemned throughout the country and the angry crowd shouted slogans like *Lal Kile ko tod do* (Raze the Red Fort), Azad Hind Fauj ko chhod do (Keep away from the INA). The then Viceroy, Lord Wavell had to use his privilege and condone the death sentence. I came to know about these only after independence."

"And where were you taken, Amma?" I had asked her, "what were you accused of?"

"I was taken to an unknown island in the deep sea.."

"For what crime?"

"For helping Netaji, who had been declared a war criminal, to reach safely to Russia."

"Did Netaji go to Russia?" I asked, "but, we had read that he was killed in a plane crash."

"O Beti, don't try to tax your mind whether he was martyred, or died, or murdered or went to Russia...If I tell you the truth, it would be betrayal to him, whom I regard as god, as I am committed to him." She changed the topic, "I was arrested for being the spy of the INA."

"Had you spied for the INA?"

Oh, no...I didn't know about spying. I had just wiped out my sindoor, as I came to know that Srikant was planning to murder Netaji, who was my sworn brother..And, Netaji was informed about certain things that I came across along with Saraswati Rajamani and other colleagues, but that was not spying, but..."

"How and why were you deported to that unknown island, Andaman Island?"

"I don't know which was the unknown island, where I had been taken to..." now, it appeared that Amma was trying to conceal things or she was not comfortable in revealing those things and she had been trying to rest.

❑

14.

"All right, Amma, you should rest," I said to her and closing her eyes, she lay down. Hardly had she taken a nap for half an hour, when she opened her eyes and asked us to take her to the washroom, we took her there, but she came back without easing herself and fell down on the bed exhausted and started babbling, though we tried to calm her down, but she continued babbling, "Japan had lost...they had laid down their arms..our military hospitals, camps had all been seized by the enemy..first, as a captive, I was brought to Calcutta..there are a number of small as well as large islands about 800 kms away from Calcutta. These islands abound in coconut trees and have a large deer population, as along with deer, predatory animals like lions, tigers and leopards were not released on these islands, who could have killed these for food. This entire island is a natural port. During the freedom struggle, this island was considered to be 'an inhospitable land for humans'. This place receives rains for eight months, as such only those who are well accustomed for lengthy spells of rains can stay here. And that is what happened there...apart from the generations of erstwhile prisoners, Bengalis and Tamilians form the majority in these islands. But, Hindi is the prime language of the population. Rain water is harvested and pooled in a vast reservoir and it is supplied to the population there."[13]

"Amma, are tribals not inhabiting these islands?"

"Where did the tribals of these islands vanish? You have posed a complex question. Tribals belonging to Aangi and Jarwa tribes used to live there. These semi-nude people were fishermen and were adept in hunting with bows and arrows. Now they live quite away from the populated areas and a few of them might be living in colonies, but it may be difficult to identify them, as they are no more semi-clad and have mingled with the locals. Moreover, very few aboriginals have been left and that too far away from the local inhabitants."

"But how their number kept dwindling, this in itself is a mystery. One of the reasons is the prevalence of venereal diseases among them, which had been a gift of the lust of the British who visited these islands. Then, they were exploited to the extreme. Thus, at present there are a few survivors left. The British exterminated these people. There are some aboriginals left in deep forests on these islands, the estimated number of these people is around 500."

"How were you transported to a far away awful island?"

"We were crammed like cargo and other lifeless things in the basement of a ship and we were even fettered and kept under strict vigilance armed guards."

"You are vegetarian, had the captives been provided vegetarian food on that ship?"

"There was no separate arrangement for vegetarian Hindu prisoners."

"Then how could they survive under such conditions..had they started eating non-veg food?"

"In emergent situations, one has to compromise.." Heaving a deep sigh, she said, "either you have to survive on roasted grams or take the food prepared by the Muslim sailors on board. A number of prisoners never observe any regimen as regard to food, but I never ate beef."

"But, had you ever consumed meat other than beef?"

"Yes, Beti, because if I could survive, then I might be able to make my contribution in the fight for freedom. But, now, when I contemplate, I fail to understand the difference between meat of pigeon and that of a calf. People go astray from the path of religion in vain.

"So, was it during the voyages that people's faith was corrupted by making them eat meat, not earlier while in jails..?" I had asked her, "What was your experience of Calcutta jail, prior to the voyage?"

"While I was in Calcutta jail, we were lodged in the cells, where other women politicians were kept or used to be kept. We were locked in these cells at 10 at night and no mat or blanket was provided to us. We were worried about the life waiting for us at the unknown island. However, we lay down on the naked floor and, fell asleep too. Around 12 at night a guard came to the cell and threw two blankets at us without saying a word. Falling of the blankets and rupture of sleep happened simultaneously. We felt bad, but we were happy to have blankets. But, now there was only the hurting fetters and fear of separation from Mother India."[14]

"At the day break, I was served khichadi and an ironsmith had also come to my cell. While cutting the handcuffs, he had made some scratches on my hand, but when he struck the fetters, his hammer also rammed on the bones of my feet, as if feeling the strength of my bones. Irritated, I asked him, "Are you blind that you are hitting my feet?"

"Forget your feet, I'll hit you at heart, what will you do?" He had said.

"What can I do, since I am in your captivity..." then I had spat at him, "behave, try to respect women."

The jailer had also accompanied him, who harshly said, "If you tell us whereabouts of Netaji, we shall let you go."

"He died in an air crash," I replied, "the whole world is aware of this fact."

"Netaji is alive, you are telling us a lie that he died in an air crash," the jailer said.

"Yes, Netaji is alive."

"But, where?"

"In my heart," the moment I uttered these words, the enraged jailer cried, "then, we will take out Netaji from your heart."

And, then he just meddled with my breast and tearing my blouse, he signalled the ironsmith, who returned with a big pruning shear. He took the breast ripper and tried to cut my right breast with it, but since it was not sharp enough and was blunt, it gave me unbearable pain when it squeezed my breasts, then the jailer warned me, "don't ever argue with me, next time I will cut off your breasts."

Knocking my nose with the shear, he said, "thank Queen Victoria that this shear has not been heated in the fire, otherwise it would have completely wiped out both your breasts."

"Did the English jailers perform such disgraceful acts in the Indian jails?"

"Far more horrible than these.."

"What more atrocious could have been than the breast ripper," I said, "how you were taken to the unknown island from there?"

❑

15.

"When I bluntly refused to divulge any information about Netaji, they painfully cut my fetters and after bandaging the bleeding legs, they served me khichadi in the morning. How can one eat, when one is experiencing unbearable pain? But, after I finished the breakfast, I was again fettered, but this time with heavier ones. Tinkling the fetters, I was made to go to the main gate, where a number of other women had been herded. A horse-driven wagon was also stationed beside some white guards. First, Bengali women were 'loaded' into the wagon, and then we North Indian women were asked to alight the wagon. There were some men also in the crowd, but a separate vehicle had been arranged for them. The doors of the wagon were still to be shut, when one of the ladies asked, "Sister, who are you?" As I introduced myself, they immediately bowed before with folded hands. It was such an emotional scene, words would not suffice for its narration.

"It was still dark and not a single soul was visible around. The vehicle at the jetty, which was immediately surrounded by guards armed sanguine-rifles. The door of the wagon was opened. A white officer came near the door and ordered us to come out of the wagon. As I was the last to enter the wagon, I got down first. I was put in a cage and taken to the bottom compartment of the ship. My handcuffs were removed, but the heavy iron fetters were still hurting me. There were three holes in the cage and it had an iron lid on the top. After repeated requests, a sepoy came to the rescue and he opened the lid.

"There, I came to know that two batches of male political prisoners had already been taken, who were handcuffed and were firmly held by a large iron chain to deter them from behaving violently. But women were provided some relief.. since any kind of mischief was not expected from us. However when we started singing patriotic songs, we were stopped. Fearful of things to come, I was sitting in a corner of the cage. When our ship reached the deep sea, we met with a pleasant surprise; our fetters were cut, but while cutting the fetters, they had somewhat ruptured our skin also and they also tried to badly touch our bodies. We, women had become the means of their entertainment. If we tried to oppose them, they would threaten to sever our flesh along with the fetters. Young women with more shapely and firm breasts were tortured the most and such women had to pay a price for their adolescence to their captors, and act as per their wishes. The sepoys used to take off the blouses of the women of the age of their mothers and caress and pinch their breasts. They made them bear this torture in silence and...

Even after tolerating such atrocities and insults, I had started singing 'sar faroshi ki tamanna' after finishing the 'Vande Mataram' which says:

'Sarfaroshi ki tamanna ab hamre dil mein hai
dekhna hai zor kitna bazue-qatil mein hai.
Rahrave rahe-muhabbat rah na jana rah mein,

lazzat-e-sahra-navardi doori-e-manzil mein hai.
Ab na agle valvle hain aur na armanon ki bheed,
ab to mit jane kin hasrat ik dile-Bislmil mein hai.
Aaj maktal mein voh qatil kah raha hai bar-bar,
kya shauk-e-shahadat bhi kisi ke dil mein hai.
Waqt aane de bata doonga tujhe e asman,
hum abhi se kya bataen kya hamare dil mein hai.
Ai shaheed-e-mulko-millat mein tere ooper nisar,
ab teri himmat ka charcha gair ki mahfil mei hai.[15]

Our heart has the dire desire to die,
See! how much force killers apply.
Let the time come we will tell O Sky!
What to tell now what we are to try.

Hope of dy'ing has dragged us here,
Landlovers' rush has increased high.

We dedicate to thee everything O Nation!
Our deeds of dare they will notify.

Neither is there any zeal or wish,
The heart of 'Bismil' now wants to die.

After this poem, I had started humming another poem of the poet, which carried unparalleled revolutionary passion:

'Mit gaya jab mitne wala phir salam aaya to kya?
dil ki barbadi ke baad unka payam aaya to kya?
Kaash apni zindagi mein hum yeh manzar dekhte,
yaun sare turbat koi mahsharkharam aaya to kya?
Mit gain jumla umeedein, jata raha sara khayal,
us ghadi jab namavar payam lekar aaya to kya.
E dil-e-nakaam mit ja ab to kuche yar mein,
phir teri nakamiyon ke bad kam aaya to kya.
Aakhri shab deed ke kabil thi Bismil ki tadap,
subahe dam gar koi bhi balay baam aaya to kya.'[16]

What's the use hats off, when the person died,
What's the use of message which came after tide.
When hopes were dead and died every thought,
What's the use of message if the messenger brought.
O Heart! go away from here and destroy thy notion,
What's the use of it if thou did after motion.
Alas! had we seen our "goal" alive,
What's the use of it, if achieved after life.
Worth seen were the last moments of 'Bismil',
What's the use if the people saw it after thrill.

"Singing and publication of this song had been banned. But, it was surprising to note that a copy of this poem was illegally made available to the 'Awadh Akhabar' by the Magistrate, Einuddin. Like 'Vandemataram' of 'Anandmath' and other hundreds of patriotic songs, each word of this poem cries of the desire to martyr oneself for the nation. These were the songs that had caught the imagination of the common man and that were the inspiration behind the revolutionaries who had spent their youth in death cells or who were hanged or died while observing satyagraha.

"As the voyage was progressing, I was singing such patriotic songs and kept on looking out of windows to catch a glimpse of the Ganges. At about 11, a woman prisoner standing beside the window announced that India had been left behind and was no more visible. Hearing this, all of us paid our obeisance to Mother India. Sea shore on one side was out of our vision, while there appeared some shadows on the other side of the shore. Our hearts were filled with grief, as the motherland for which we had left our families and beloved ones, had moved away from us and we were not sure whether we would be able to return to the motherland or not.

Somehow, I managed to calm my emotions and I remembered a few lines of poet Bismil:

haay jananee janmabhoomi
chhodakar jaate hain ham
dekhana phir kab vaapas
lautakar aate hain ham[17]

'O Motherland! We are leaving you,
but, let us see when we return.'

Suddenly, an officer came to our cell and staring at us with ill intention, warned us, "If you remember mother or your motherland, I'll strip you of your clothes and will throw you out in the sea."

Thereafter, there was silence for quite a long time and we were unaware, as where we were or where we were heading to. When we regained our senses, and we looked outside, Mother India had gone out of sight and as far as our sight could go, we could see a wide expanse of water. When we could not see anything else, we went back to our places and sat silently. After sometime, suddenly three or four persons entered the cage after opening the lock. All of us became uneasy as we were fearful that these persons might molest us. They stared at us. There was evil in their eyes, but we saw large bags in their hands and they were looked like village peddlers. Before we could speak, they asked us, 'take these and have your meals.'

It was a pleasant surprise for us and we picked up our vessels...India has a long tradition of being respectful to food, but since the country was enslaved, mother and food has always been disrespected. Our captors had provided us roasted grams, chiwada, salt, chillies, tamarind and sugar. It was also the time for food and we were also hungry, but who would eat so much food? A question came to my mind...a few grams of sugar was good, but who is going to eat rotten chiwda and foul smelling grams. I thought for a few moments and then suddenly I remembered of water, but that too was limited..even then we washed chiwda with the water, but in vain. Those who were expecting to eat chiwda with sugar, were also disappointed as the sugar was also wasted. Grams with tamarind and salt gave us some relief from hunger. We asked the sentries a number of times to provide us something edible and asked them, "Call your Captain..we don't want to eat such rotten food."

Our request fell on deaf ears and he said, "Since you had refused to dance before the Captain in your birthday suits, you do not even deserve such food."

"Listen, we are political prisoners, not prostitutes," when I replied, he said, "it is just tit for tat; you did not satiate the captain's hunger, then how can you expect that he will provide food to you hungry women?"

I thought it better to keep quiet, as it was no use arguing with them. I also decided not to plead with such persons.

Next day, a Muslim woman prisoner came to me and said, "Sister, take my share of grams, since you are vegetarian.."

"How will these three handfuls help me?"

A Muslim havildar, standing nearby said, "Mother, if you are willing to eat food prepared by us, then we can offer you some food."

Expressing my gratitude, I opened up and said, "Some Muslims like you are benevolent by nature, but there appears to be an inherent desire in you to defile Hindus by offering them food prepared by you..."

"Madam, you are blaming us..."

"I have just spoken the truth," I said, "all right, give us your food, but remember that Aryans are so strong that such food will not pollute them."

"A Nepali Havildar was also listening to our talks, he thought that hunger had forced me to spoil my other worldly prospects. Then I accepted rice from them without any argument, but on one condition, that they would not question me regarding Netaji.

"Leaving the land behind, when the ship 'Maharaja' picked up speed, I started losing my balance and the rapid movement of the ship had been tossing me, and I started vomiting. Making fun of me, a sentry said, "We never knew that you had become pregnant..who is the lucky one? Tell us about him."

"You wretched! Call the doctor, I am dying."

"So what? Your death would reduce the number of passengers and your dead body would be thrown into the sea. We don't keep a record of you, that you have been travelling on this ship."

Nobody cared about us..but when my condition started worsening, lime juice was brought, which gave me some relief. But during this hour of crisis, I was surrounded by satans, only my God was by my side. Though the lime juice provided relief, but a new problem cropped up. There were two wooden tubs in the cage, in which I had been kept, which were being used as latrines. Now the stinking smell from these tubs had become unbearable. Not only we, but the guards, who had been insulting us and making fun of us, were also reeling in that stinking odour. One of them had remarked, "This is the first time that I have been put on duty on Maharaja, had I known about such conditions, I wouldn't have joined the service of the British."

"It is not service, but it is slavery," I corrected him, "you are slaves of the British and I am fighting a war to liberate crores of people like you...yet you are behaving..."

The guard had softened a little and said, "Sister, please forgive me...you are a large-hearted woman...You are a goddess, we treated you so badly, but you never said harsh words to us, but you cursed the British."

Then, they started describing their sufferings, now it appeared that everyone was distressed in himself and being in pain and sorrow, none of us could realize when the sun had come up. I could not resist looking at the rising sun.

Suddenly, I saw a ball of light rising slowly out of the sea. There was water, unfathomed water all around. We were having a feeling of eternity. The sun was rising on one side, whereas the eternal man had become visible on the other side. As if, there was a congruence of knowledge and deeds. Devotion and yoga were assimilating. During the sunrise in the midst of the deep sea, I noticed a strange phenomenon. I saw that suddenly the ball of light which was appearing lying on the surface of the sea, got released from the surface of the sea."[18]

The sun shone like a red ball in the sky and that made me realize that if we had to liberate our country, then we would have also to do something like the sun rising from the sea and soaring to the sky. Now, we were able to see huts on the islands. We were also seeing semi-clad fishermen on their boats catching fish. I was surprised to see that prisoners on these uninhabited islands had also been provided with clothes, because I was told that I would be thrown naked on some such island, if I did not divulge the whereabouts of Netaji."

I had asked Amma, "Did you believe that they would behave so shamefully and throw you on some unknown island in the sea?"

"There was no reason to disbelieve such treatment."

"Did they ever stoop to such behaviour?"

"Why only they," Amma continued, "we were treated even by those Japanese, who had helped us raise the Indian National Army..they too had stabbed us in the back."

"What are you saying, Amma?"

"I am telling you the truth," filled with emotions, Amma went on, "When after taking off from Sri Lanka, the Brtish bombers had started destroying the Japanese ships, the Japanese suspected that Indians on seized islands were involved in spying for the British. As a consequence thousands of Indians were made prisoners and were thrown in jails. When the British pressure mounted and the foodgrain crises lead to starvation, the enraged Japanese did a horrifying act on Havlok island to save their lives."

"What was that?"

"They had crammed more than 700 Indians on three ships and after hitting them with butts of their guns, had thrown those alive Indians into the sea and 44 Indians were gunned down in their headquarters on Raas Island. After fiercely attacking the Japanese and making them flee, the British warriors had captured the Andaman Island. In the meanwhile, with the dropping of the nuclear bomb by Americans over Hiroshima and Nagasaki, the world was shaken. After massacre of millions of humans and creatures, there was a truce with a global treaty. Meanwhile, Britain had also withdrawn its 'Penal Code Act', which had allowed it to take the offenders prisoners and they released all the Indian prisoners. The hearing at the Red Fort also acquitted the soldiers of the INA. Ram Singh, Sardar Singh Toofan, Umrao Singh, Sirdare, were all acquitted...but what was my fault that I was not brought to Delhi, why was I not tried in Delhi? Why was I first, kept as a prisoner at Calcutta and when I didn't give a statement as per their wishes and not opened my mouth about Netaji's whereabouts, why was I being taken to an unknown Island or to an unknown jail or cellular jail or any torture cell nearby...I failed to understand.

❑

16.

For three days and three nights, munching grams and chiwda and often vomiting, I felt as if my guts were coming out. Throwing me out on an inhabited island, meant nothing to me, as within a short time I would have been dead, along with my dreams of independence, but the desire to free my country was keeping me alive. The dream of freedom was the biggest spiritual power for me. Moments of freedom are heavenly for everybody.

Enduring three days and three nights on the ship, at last, we reached an island, which appeared beautiful from a distance. Rows of coconut trees and bungalows of officials looked like beautiful framed pictures. But who knows the inside story of these bungalows? There was a building at a distance. The sepoy announced, "This is the jail."

The ship anchored at the port. Doctors examined me. Then I alighted from the ship, but I had to pass the distance amidst the tinkering of iron fetters and baggage on my head. When I entered the jail, I met a dwarfish stocky white man, who said, "You have not come here on a honeymoon, but to serve a sentence, don't ever try to flee from this place,

as it is surrounded with miles and miles of water and the jungles abound with tribals with poisonous arrows, and who are enemies and hostile to man, that is why a lion becomes a lamb here.

❑

17.

I had a feeling of environ of a deserted cremation ground in that jail on that inhabited island. There were separate arrangements for keeping the women prisoners and the row of barracks, where our cell was, housed with women and children. The first atrocity after our medical check up was that our heads were shaved. When we protested that among Hindus, only the widow's, heads are shaved, the barber said, "You have killed your husband, then why shouldn't you be a widow?"

I was speechless to hear this, as to how this barber came to know about my killing of the traitor husband. But, no one listened to us and heads of all the women were shaved, I felt as if the British had shaved our heads, because these foreigners are about to leave our country. A coarse and rough dhoti was given to us, which could hardly cover the knees. After changing our clothes, we were asked to go inside with two blankets and an iron dish and bowl, and we were told, "You are reaping what you have sown. You are most dangerous offenders, but our Queen Victoria is very merciful, as she has asked us to be lenient to women prisoners. As such, you will have to do women-like light work of sewing clothes for prisoners, making baskets, grinding food grains, etc."

After that, the women who had accompanied me, were sent to the hospital for 10 days. In fact, prisoners brought here, were initially sent to hospital for ten days, where they were looked after, if they had any ailment, but I was an exception to the rule. I was allotted the work of grinding from the day one.

When I refused to work, the lady guard asked me, "Why are you not working?"

"Why was I not sent to hospital for 10 days, like the other prisoners?"

"O, Maharani! Have you come to your husband's house, come and start the work."

"I won't do it."

"Why not?"

"My pleasure."

"Your pleasure won't work here," she burst out in anger, "if you don't work, the jailer Bari, the God of this prison, will punish you, which will make you plead for death."

"I don't care."

Immediately, I was taken to the jailer.

Bari Saheb spoke, "Why are you not working?"

"Am I a servant that I should work here?"

"You are a wicked woman."

"Wicked are you and wicked is your father."

"You, worthless woman, you call me wicked," the enraged jailer was about to get up, when I pounced on him and pushed his chair backward and punched and kicked him on his stomach. When he tried to regain his posture and to attack me, I again punched two or three blows on his face. He must have been a very mean and awful person, because, persons from his office were laughing, when he was being beaten.

Then I was held by guards and abusing me the jailer said that I was a very wicked woman. He tore my clothes..with shame, I turned to face the wall, but those cruel persons started whipping my naked back..and tied my hands and continued whipping, till a gentleman came to my rescue. There was a hospital nearby, Dr. Dumpala Malli Reddy was a loyal person, who had come to that place after hearing the commotion. He scolded the jailer Bari, "this woman came here yesterday, I hadn't examined her, then how did you dare to allot her work? And, after calling her here, you are beating her. Look, her clothes are wet with blood and she has been hit in her eye, you are torturing prisoners at your will."

They were subdued with the doctor's rebuke. He took me to the hospital, bandaged my eye and put me in a cell nearby.

The doctor asked me, "why did you kill your husband for an ordinary goon? Was Netaji Subhas your lover?"

"Mind your language, doctor," I roared with rage.

"I want freedom, freedom for my country, that is why I killed my husband...he was a British supporter like you, a wretched pimp."

"Shanti...Shanti...(calm down, calm down)."

"I'm not Shanti, my name is Neera." The irritated doctor left and as a punishment, I didn't get my dinner in that hospital cell."[19]

❑

18.

Sharp stomachs make short devotion, then how could I sleep? I remained awake the whole night, and then the intermittent call 'Jagte Raho' made my vain efforts to sleep worthless. Hundreds of watchmen with hurricane lanterns in their hands were keeping vigil the whole night. These watchmen were also made to fan the overseer of the jail. May there be rain or some other obstacle, the fanning must continue standing in the open. I had realized this one night, as it rained that night and these persons had not moved from their positions. Once, the guard, who was fanning, felt drowsy, the senior overseer pulled the rope and abused the guard and as punishment, he was given[12] lashes on that night. I could also hear calls by four guards in the hospital. The outside gate was under the strict watch of watchmen and every three hours there was a change of guards. In case, any guard fall ill, the line guard was to report to the watch tower guard who in turn was to report to the prisoner guard of the number one middle line. That watchman would call the hospital watchman, and similarly information would pass on to the gate watchman. This watchman would call the head warden, who then would go to the compounder inside the jail for taking the medicine, that would be brought to the watch tower guard and then it would reach the prisoner. If any prisoner tried to commit suicide due to the torturous treatment, the information about it would travel the same route. Suicide is not a solution, security and independence can only be possible by amending the penal code. A large number of prisoners and guards could not walk long distances. But, they would show the light standing at a place. Only two lights used to be placed in each line, which means that there was one lamp each at the ends of the line.

❑

19.

The so-called protectors of human rights, were themselves breaking these rights to pieces. There was no light in prisoners' cells and except for two-three cells in the beginning, all the other cells were devoid of pots for urinating. For a bath and washing of clothes, saline water of the sea was made available to us. Instead of cleaning the utensils, the saline water was making these more rusty. There was a drinking water tap, but the water was scarcely available. During the rains, water was harvested under the tin sheds. If the technician supplying water was a kind-hearted or good-natured man, he would supply drinking water, otherwise, only one pound of water was supplied. Earlier, the saline water was treated and made potable, but the engine was less powerful and the cost was too high! So, he used to supply us with the saline sea water. In the jail, all the castes were to take water from a common tank, which was of 1x10 yards in size. While taking a bath, waste water used to fall on the other person. Brahmin women were upset, but the water of the jail was no less than nectar for them.[20]

One day, when a utensil of a Brahmin touched me, she said, "You, wretched woman, you have desecrated my utensil," and threw her pot away. Then, I held her tightly with both my hands and after releasing her, I said, "look, I have desecrated you, why don't you throw away your body? It is for people like you that we have to undergo slavery..when the foreigners used to heap atrocities on people of a particular caste, loot them, then people of other castes used to make fun of them due to this evil of untouchability. They failed to realize tomorrow they could be the next (bari-turn) victims of such atrocities."

"Bari," uttering this word, she was frightened, may be this reminded her of Bari, the jailer.

❑

20.

I was allotted neither the sewing task not the weaving baskets, but considering my crime to be most heinous, I was tasked to pound paddy to make rice. Though there were crushers for pounding the paddy, but I had to pound the paddy with the old method of manual pounding and grinding wheat on a hand-operated grinding mill.

One day, I had arguments with the jailer, "Why am I supposed to do a man's task?"

"You have killed your husband and call yourself a woman, you bitch."

For lighter arguments, I was lashed and I was yoked to the crusher and was forced to extract 30 pounds of oil on that day."

❑

21.

There was a tin shed with cubicles in our jail which were used as latrines. Only seats were screened with tin strips leaving way for entering the cubicle. This latrine shed could be used by ten women simultaneously. As soon as a batch of ten women was allowed to enter the cubicles, another batch of 10 women was asked to stand before the cubicles. I was among the women who had committed heinous crimes. Women in batches of six were secured with a moving chain round a pulley that moved round our feet and when any one of us had to go to the latrine, all of us had to move along. And thus, on the pretext of going to the latrine, we were punished and we never understood the rationale of this chain gang punishment.

In that jail, six months of chain gang punishment was meted out for insignificant things. Not only this, the sentence was extended for another six months. It used to be an unending punishment, which kept extending like the tail of Hanuman. Chain gang prisoners were assigned laborious tasks. Neither were we allowed to wear our usual clothes nor were we permitted to demand anything. During illness too, we had to wear the jail uniform and could never dream of having brass utensils. Others were condoned (on the occasion of the Coronation), but we unfortunates were not allowed to have such privileges.

Women were made to work even in menstrual periods, however, there was some relief during those days, as they were given lighter tasks like sewing, embroidering or weaving baskets. But, there was no relief from pounding grains in such periods. Each woman was given 15 coconut shells, whereas in the male section of the jail the inmates were given 20 shells.[21] These shells were to be made soft, by pounding the shells placed on a wooden plank with a wooden pounder. As the shell was soft, it was pealed and then after soaking it in water, it was pounded again. In the process, chaff was separated and the fibres were made into bundles after drying these in the sun. We had to make bundles of approximately one kilogram daily. In the beginning, it was difficult to understand, what all this was about. When we started the task, blisters grew on our hands. After toiling for the whole day, only about 100 grams of fibres could be made. When at three in the afternoon, we went to submit the work done by us, I was astonished when we were showered with abuses and were instructed to follow the hard rules of widowhood.

❑

22.

Women prisoners were also made to satiate the lust of Bari and his petty officers, as if these rascals had no mother and sisters in their homes. If anyone dared to refuse to act against their will, she was even hanged or her private parts were filled with chillies. If any woman prisoner tried to protest and picked up stones to throw at the aggressor (since there was no weapon to defend oneself, victim women would often pick up stones in self-defence. In case, any implement like an axe or spade was at hand, it could also be used for defence), such a stone was weighed and the offender woman was told that had she struck with such a heavy stone (more than one pound of weight), the other person would have died. And the weight of that stone was enough evidence before the law and such a woman, who had intended to kill, was hanged.

Some women were tasked to bring dried wood and honey from the forest. If anyone tried to escape or hide in the forest, guards were asked to bring back her beheaded head or she was paraded naked before all the prisoners and sometimes, a tribal was made to rape her.

❑

23.

India is a country of multi religions and the followers have different ways of worshipping their gods, but the supreme religion is that of humanity. To raise one's voice against the sufferings of others or atrocities being heaped on oneself, is also a religion. I was tired of the inhuman treatment in the jail, so I decided to lodge my protest against such atrocities. One day, when the junior jailer came on an inspection visit to our barrack, I confronted him with folded hands and said, "Sir, there is a request."

The junior jailer stopped, but being unable to understand my language, he asked his colleagues, "What is this lady saying?"

An overseer of the station was also among the inspection team. Addressing the lady guard, he asked, "Isn't she the crazy Neera, the killer of her husband?"

"Sir, you are right," the lady guard replied, "she is the same insane Neera, who always chatters like this."[22]

So, he told the junior jailer that I was a mad person and was in the habit of talking rubbish, whenever she sees an officer. This explanation made all of them laugh and they left the cell. Immediately, I was handcuffed and locked in my cell. Within no time, I was slapped with a case and was accused of talking irrelevantly and was sentenced for six months as chain gang and 20 cane-strikes on my naked back. I protested and told them to respect women, because had there been no woman, this entire universe would have been deserted like the moon and all of them too, would not have been there. But they were entirely devoid of having regard for women!

❑

24.

Neat and clean attire radiates a look of youthfulness and act as camouflage for old age. But in this jail, there was no camouflage for your youth, but here, the jailer and all his stooges were plunderers of youth...the madness of youth makes a person blind. But, if he takes the path of benevolence, he could achieve a vision, and the jailer needed such a vision, but that devil was miles away from kindness and benevolence...he was just obeying the orders of his superiors. I had never been careless about my body, as carelessness is more dangerous than ignorance.

One day, I suddenly felt the start of menstruation, and I had to go to the washroom, leaving my task unfinished. That was the only place, on the pretext of which, I could leave my seat, but the jailer was immediately informed about my absence from work, and I was accused of revolting in the jail and taken to the torture chamber for punishment. There was a triangular wooden post, which had a pulley, through which a rope was hanging. My right hand was tied to that rope and I was pulled upward. Now I was hanging on my right hand on that rope, then my left hand was tied with my left ankle. My body was hanging with the rope in a triangular shape, a

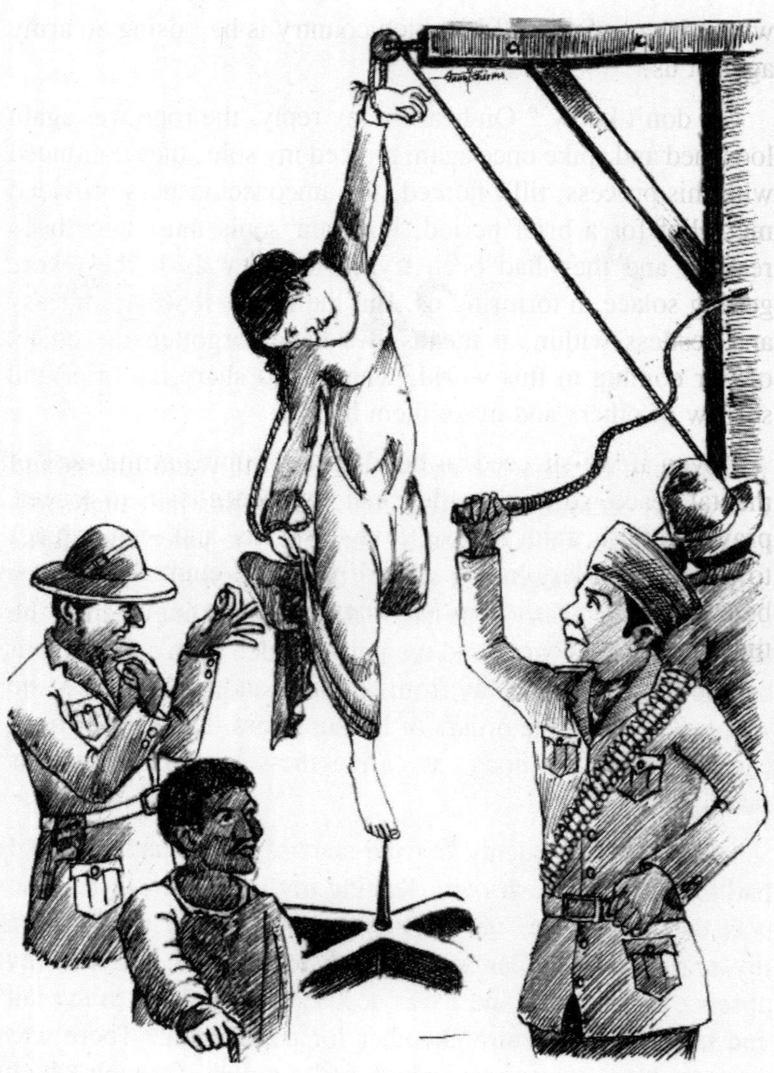

wooden square frame with a protruding iron spike had been placed below my right foot. Suddenly the rope on that pulley was loosened and the sole of my foot was pierced with the spike and I cried out of pain. Then, Bari asked me, "Tell me, where is your Subhas? In which country is he raising an army against us?"

"I don't know." On hearing my reply, the rope was again loosened and spike once again pierced my sole..they continued with this process, till I fainted..this unconsciousness provided me relief for a brief period, but their souls must have been restless and they had been trying to show as if they were getting solace in torturing us. But the fact is if we are uneasy and restless within, it means, we have forgotten the object of our coming to this world, which is to share the grief and sorrow of others and make them happy.

Even if we succeed in building an empire at the cost of mental peace, still we are defeated, as silence leads to prayer, prayer to faith, faith to love, love to service and service leads to peace. A ruler should achieve peace through service and benevolence, but the British Empire was miles away from these divine tenets....

❑

25.

Why were we made to suffer the atrocious slavery? It was the result of misdeeds of our Rajas and Maharajas. In fact misfortunes take the way, which we ourselves keep open for them. We, ourselves had invited the dependence... Jaichand was one of us, but whom should I have blamed? Whenever I wanted to find faults, I used to consider my own vices. Standing near another woman prisoner, I was engaged in my own thoughts, when suddenly I started laughing; Bari thought that both of us were talking and I must be laughing at him.

The tyrant of the jail, Bari turned towards me and asked, "Why do you talk in Bangla, talk in Hindustani."

"I don't know Hindustani, the mixture of Hindi and Urdu."

"Aren't you talking in Hindustani, now?"

Fear also fears fearlessness. This fearlessness was in my genes, so I said to him in plain Meerut dialect, "You wicked person (kamina), what would you do, if I speak Hindustani?" Perhaps, he couldn't understand my words, but he was

enraged and shouted at me, "You wretched woman! So, you don't understand, I'll have to break your bones."[23]

Bari was also a hunter of crows. Sometimes, he used to kill dogs and when the population of cats exceeded in the jail, he used to get them thrown into the sea, crammed them in jute bags. He used to get satisfaction in killing dogs and cats. He was mentally just a killer of dogs and cats, then how could he deal with a lioness like me? He wanted me to be tamed, that is why I was taken to the torture cell after a while. There was a big hand-operated fodder-shredder like wooden equipment with a large wheel, with a wider rim. I was tied on that wheel and it was rotated violently. I also was being rotated and within two rounds how many of my 206 bones had cracked, I had no idea. I had fainted and when I regained consciousness, I found myself naked. When I looked at my naked body,[24] I realized that the British Officers completely lacked morality. In fact, morality is a crucial addiction. The British pretended to be patrons of principles and morality, but they never followed these in their real lives. A person, who boasts of morality, but does not follow such ethics in his life, is not a human, he is a devil. Each and every historical event leaves its indelible print, which inspires the new generation in writing a new history. Amidst such limitless atrocities, I never lost my patience, because I knew, it is the person, who keeps patience, is the ultimate winner and devoid of self-restraint, a person loses everything.

❑

26.

Saving a drowning person, is the duty of a good human being. The aim of my fight for freedom was to save the Indians drowning in the sea of dependence. But the rulers had considered me an enemy of humanity and rulers. However, on that day all limits were crossed, when in the darkness of the night, I was taken out of the jail and brought to the shore of the island. In our village, I had seen dhenkli (water-lifting appliance), which was used for lifting water for irrigation of the fields. Here on the shore, I saw a large iron dhenkli. The dhenkli in our village had a large leather bowl tied at the end, which was dipped into the water and then the water-filled bowl was upturned into a drain, which took the water to the fields for irrigation. But here, instead of a bowl, a chair was tied to the end. I was forcibly put on that chair and tied tightly. Then the jailer asked, "Where is Subhas?" I had repeatedly been asked just one question and my reply had always been, "In an air accident, he..."

"You bitch! Telling lies again, you have been telling lies again and again, since you have come here..you are repeating the lie of his death in an air crash and not telling the truth that he had been sent to Russia."

"No, Netaji is not in Russia.:

"Then, where is he?"

"I had told you already..."

"Died...now you too die" and torturous dhenkli was loosened from the other end and the chair along with me went down in the water with a splash. I thought that this was the end of me, but then they lifted that apparatus out of the water and I was once again asked, "Who are the other persons, apart from Subhas, who are trying to raise the INA?"

"There is nothing like that."

"No, you are again telling a lie, because Karan Singh Tomar of your Guhandi Bawali Badaut, has told us otherwise, he was also taken to this island as a prisoner along with you."

"You are telling a lie...That Jat would prefer to die rather than rebel against Netaji." Hearing this from me, they once again dipped me into the water and then the game of see-saw was repeatedly played till I lost my consciousness. When I came to my senses, I was lying naked on the floor and all my tormentors were drinking and laughing like devils.

Crying in pain, I asked, "What have you done to me during my unconscious state?"

As I said this, they again started their devilish laugh... suddenly my hand reached between my legs, I was shocked. I was bleeding and the ground underneath was covered with my blood. It was enough to realize as to what had happened. I gathered my torn clothes and walked staggeringly towards the hillock nearby, their eyes were following me. Then I heard whispering from behind and when I looked behind, I found accompanied with other officers, Bari was following me. He asked abusively of me, "Have you come here to commit suicide?"

"I am not that weak, that I would commit suicide."

"All right. Then let us commit your suicide.." and Bari forcefully hit my breast with the butt of his rifle and I fell into the sea from the height of the hill to meet my death. The water splashed with full force and I was enveloped in it and after that I don't remember what fate I had met with. Had the sea creatures gobbled me? How did I meet my death? Earth is constantly changing, but the soul and eternal soul are still and firm. One should, therefore do such deeds which lead to the soul merging with the eternal soul. Perhaps, my soul was struggling to merge with the eternal soul. As whatever bad might have happened to me, but my deeds were good.

❑

27.

Circumstances transform life and the life too has the power to transform the circumstances. That is why we say that a man should not be a slave to circumstances, but man should be able to control circumstances. As such, when I regained consciousness, I felt that nothing is impossible...but soon I came out of the reveries, because having considered me dead, I found myself in hell. Wonder is the base of worship and it was the first step in the direction of reaching him. His universe is full of wonders and these wonders lead us to philosophy, because I considered myself to be worthy of heaven and not of hell, where I had found myself.

This hell was in a small island in the midst of the sea and it was surrounded by a dense forest. Temperament, restraint and patience are a panacea for every ill, and now these three traits were my strength. Many naked persons of that hell had surrounded me. Young and old women, children, youth and older men were all naked. A woman was sprinkling water on my face and was speaking in a strange language. Neelu taganda, she was saying with water in her palm...I thought, she was asking me, if I would like to take water. I thought that the word Neelu is the corrupt form of the Sanskrit word

Neer, meaning water. Now I realized that I was not dead and was not in hell, but I was alive and was amidst mysterious primitive tribals, who were unknown to the world. These naked, small hair on their heads, with pointed reddish nose and iron arrows in their hands and holding blazing torches even during the day, appeared to me as aliens. Seeing me regaining consciousness, a strong man with a spear rushed towards me and was about to pierce my chest, when another man stopped him and women with mouths agape started crying 'paa uf..paa uf'. I understood that they were saying in their language 'keep away evil...keep away evil.'

I had a feeling that they had not saved my life, but they belonged to a men eater tribe and were fighting among each other to have the first right over my flesh. I was thrown into the sea to die, whereas these people took me out from the sea, to have one day's meal. I thought that I was the most fortunate person, as my flesh would provide food to these people. Though fight for freedom of my country would remain unfulfilled, still I considered it to be a great achievement if my flesh would satiate their hunger and my bones would provide them material for their arms for protection.

With folded hands, I surrendered to them...and started uttering 'Om'..but hearing me uttering 'Om', they immediately folded their hands and started saying 'Hom..hom', they were saying 'hom' instead of 'Om' and started putting their burning torches in a pool and some women plucked flowers and petals and started making offerings to me. They started singing a strange lyric... suryammarave... devammarave... Ippade... povaddu...now I came to understand their language a little, which to me appeared to be a mixture of Sanskrit, Tamil, and Telugu. At that moment a fighter plane passed over the island

and they started shooting their fiery arrows in the sky...I could realize that they are adept at firing missiles.

What an unfortunate woman I was! Instead of killing me, they had started worshipping me, as if I was a goddess. Fire used to be kindled before me, which they considered as divine fire and I was offered eggs of turtles, semi-cooked fish, earth worms, etc. to eat.[25] They also offered me worms from the peeled oysters, which reminded me of peeling and eating of ground nuts during childhood. But I was a vegetarian, however I couldn't remain vegetarian in the torture cell, where I was made to eat even beef and both my soul and body had been defiled. But mentally, I felt restless for the freedom of my country, as such my soul within said, "accept whatever they offer you to eat...what is the use of such a person, who conquers the world, but fails to identify one's own soul. The inner voice is the divine voice".

They had taken care of my hunger, provided me hospitality, as such they were praiseworthy people. They praised me that I had alienated myself from the British, whereas I silently praised these tribals who had kept themselves aloof from the wicked world and had maintained their freedom. But I was happy..I was now amidst my own, amidst the tribals of my country who were as hateful of the British, as I was. Now they were my friends.

Those who stand by you in sorrow, are real friends. Everyone claims to be a friend in sunshine days, but in darker days, even one's shadow disappears. But the tribals of this island had proved to be my friends in need. I was, therefore free under their patronage and I had a mission to lead my countrymen towards independence, as such I had compromised and accepted the food provided by these people.

Prosperity is a great teacher, whereas calamities inspire one to struggle for achieving one's aim. But, here amidst these tribals, I had taken them as my own, though I had certain reservations over their traditions. But need doesn't follow rules, but violates every rule immediately. Something like this happened with me. I needed those people, as such I had violated many rules related to my eating habits and clothing requirements.

The place, which initially I had taken for hell, had turned into a heaven for me during my stay for a few days there. There were coconut trees in abundance and these people used to relish the coconut water. I was amidst a variety of trees of beetle nut, palm, cashew nuts, clove, mulberry and other trees which were unknown to me and which I had seen for the first time in my life; there was koo...koo of cuckoos, group songs of weaver-birds, melodious singing of birds; slow moving turtles, crocodiles, pheasants, foxes, pythons, deer, wild goats, peacocks, pigeons and many more wild lives were there; then how could one say that it was an uninhabited island, on the contrary it was such a beautiful island, which could defy even heaven. And this was the beauty of our India, that the place where hungry and naked people live has been bestowed with nature's choicest gifts. I consider it more beautiful than heaven.

I stayed there for months at a stretch. Those people treated me with their herbs, due to which I was able to regain the strength of my body. Meanwhile, I started understanding their language to some extent and I explained to them in their language that all of us are Indians and the British had made us slaves and we have to oust them from our country. I, therefore need to leave their island. This made the people of this small island very sad, their eyes were filled with tears and when

I told them in their language, "Don't you think our country should be made independent? Should I not go?"

They unanimously said, "Yes, go for the freedom of the country. These tears you see in our eyes, reflect our joy that soon our country will be free..we too are living on this island in dependence...now we would be back to our roots and Satyug would come, Ramrajya would come...our elders had been saying that our forefathers had contributed to the Lanka bridge, we would witness Ramrajya again..."

I was astonished to find that Ram was still in their hearts. They built a wooden boat for me and filled it with fruits, eggs of sea creatures, worms, oysters etc., for me to eat during my journey. They were unaware of agriculture practices; as such they didn't have food grains for me. But the most important thing they gave me, were sea pearls, which must have been worth lakhs of rupees, these were priceless. Offering these, their chief had said, "Mother Goddess, we are starving people, but for centuries we live in the lap of Mother Nature and she cares for our hunger. We had learnt from our forefathers that ours is a large country, and to liberate it we would require large sums of money and we are offering you these priceless pearls, which would help you in your freedom struggle. You start a war for freedom in our country, where gods and goddesses reside, and we, here, would be sinking their ships. Come what may, we would not allow them to set foot on this small island. We may die, this island may be deserted, but we would never bow before the foreigners..."

Their patriotic feelings had moved me. I was wondering that the tribals, who had been cut off from their country for centuries, who are leading a hungry and miserable life, which had led them to become man-eaters, but they are filled with love for their motherland, Bharat, i.e. India. Staying with them for a few days had made me realize that poor people do not need our sympathy and mercy, but they deserve our love and care. They can give us much more than what we can provide them. We can find such poor people not only on this small island, but they are everywhere in our country. There are people among you, who are leading miserable lives, as they neither have anybody to love them or who call them their own. This is the real poverty. We need people, who could own them.

It was night, when I boarded the boat. As the time of departure approached, my eyes were filled with tears, whereas many of those people were sad and some of them had a smile, as they believed that a guest must be seen off with smiling faces. A smile is respite for the worn and weary; day light for dejected ones and the best gift from Nature to the miserable. This I could realize, while living with them on the island. I was bidding farewell to a silent and peaceful island. We search for God, but we can never find him with noise, power and restlessness. God is the image of silence. Look, how trees, flowers and grass grow silently. Look at the stars, the sun and the moon, how they silently watch us. Our silent prayers provide us more and can help us contributing more towards our active life. Those people living in a peaceful environment, who had been living in a thousands of years old civilization, those who do not have clothes to wear and have no knowledge of agriculture even today, are a hundred times more contented that us. We have acquired all the luxuries of the world with the help of science and knowledge, but can we call ourselves contented and happy?

They had been living on a small island in an ocean, that is why they had designed my boat so minutely, that it could survive the high and low tides. Assuring me of the safety of my boat, they had encouraged me and also provided me with an indigenous compass and map: they also kept certain herbs in my boat which were powerful repellents for dangerous sea creatures. They also provided two efficient boatmen as my co-travellers and guards. They had taken full care of my security and safety. Then they guided me about the direction in which I had to move. After a voyage of several days, my small boat landed on a shore, which was not India, but I had landed at Indonesia. After my safe landing both the tribals bade me goodbye and soon they disappeared on that sea.

❑

28.

Reaching Indonesia, I sold some of the pearls and started planning for the freedom of my country, but then I came to know about the British plan to leave India, as they had announced the independence of India, but they had put some conditions. One of the conditions was that in case after independence, Netaji Subhas Chandra Bose comes to India, he should be handed over by the Indian Government to Britain, as he was a prisoner of war and for this a time limit of 99 years was decided. It meant that if Subhas comes to India, the future government would hand him over to Britain. India got its independence on August 15, 1947. That was a golden day in the history of India, we, however, got our independence at the cost of the partition of India and the country was divided as India and Pakistan. With the advent of a new India, the entire country was eagerly waiting for the mid-night address by Nehruji at the Legislative Assembly. He said, "At the stroke of the midnight hour, India will awake to life and freedom. A moment comes, which comes but rarely in history, when we step out from the old to the new, when an age ends, and when the soul of a nation, long suppressed, finds utterance, leads to a bright future."

On that day, Pt. Jawaharlal Nehru became the first Prime Minister of independent India. Though most of the members of the Congress Executive Committee were in favour of Vallabhbhai as the Prime Minister, but Mahatma Gandhi insisted on making Nehru, the Prime Minister. Vallabhbhai had dedicated his entire life for the nation; this Iron Man had acted in this very manner for his entire life. Some people wanted Jinnah to be PM, but Nehru didn't accept Jinnah. And for this, the then Indian leadership conspired to accept the partition of India or the death of the country, for which neither I, nor the future generation would ever forgive them.

❑

29.

Indians were ecstatic, they were charged with new energy, and it was happiness all around, though the communal riots had added to the miseries of people, but they too were happy, as they knew that they had to pay a price for the independence, which they had long fought for. With the new dawn of the independence, the country was partitioned in two nations, but in India, it was still a conglomeration of more than 500 princely states. Many of the princes had willingly signed the merger documents with India, but there were some princely states, who considered themselves as an independent nation. It was Eid-ul-Adha and the Nizam of the largest princely state of South India, Hyderabad, was administering the oath of allegiance to all the respected persons of the state, gathered in the glittering diwan-e-khas of his palace. Offering sovereigns of gold wrapped in a silk scarf to the Nizam, all of them pledged their allegiance to him.

The crazy and peevish Nizam was a very fortunate person. He was one of those extravagant princes, who still ruled the state. One of the other two was the Nawab of Junagarh, who was a tyrant devoid of humanity, and the other was Maharaja Hari Singh, the ruler of heavenly Kashmir. Despite geographical limitations and beyond logic, he tried hard to merge his small state, surrounded by the Indian area, with Pakistan. His rule came to an end. The rebellion against Nawab Saheb allowed him time just for fleeing with his wives and pet dogs in a plane to Pakistan.

Hari Singh too, had tried to negotiate with Britain to grant independence to his state of Kashmir, but attack by Pakistan forced him to change his mind and he considered it better to take refuge in India, whereas the Nizam had already appealed to the United Nations Organization.

On the occasion of Eid, when his Commander-in-Chief, General Aldross offered him two sovereigns instead of one, the Hyderabad Nizam happily said, "I expected this from you, as you are the most loyal person to Hyderabad State, that is why you have offered me two instead of one sovereign."

"His Highness, I never meant this."

"Then, what is your intention?"

"Please select any one of the two."

"What do you mean?"

"My intention is clear. Time demands either you enter into an agreement with the Government of India or with Pakistan."

"You wretch! Had you not been my Commander, I would have got you beheaded right now. Even the British Court cannot interfere with my decisions."

"Kindly forgive me for my foolishness, His Highness."

"You would be pardoned only on one condition, that you will forcibly convert all the Hindus in the state into Muslims."

"Your orders will be followed in letter and spirit, Your Highness."

"That is what I expect of you."[26]

❑

30.

The citizens were against Nizam's rule in Hyderabad, but the Nizam wanted to continue as a ruler forcibly. He started committing atrocities on his subjects. At the instance of Razakar Field Marshal Qasim Rizvi, patriots were crammed into jails built in the dense forests of Telangana and were subjected to horrible torture. But, how can the voice of the masses be suppressed through oppression? More the atrocities, more violent the movement turned.

With the pronouncement of independence, the Hyderabad State banned all the nationalist organizations. The Arya Samaj was a prominent movement among the banned organizations. The Arya Samaj published a Hindi Weekly, *Milap*, whose editor was Mahatma Anand Swami and which carried reports on atrocities heaped on people by the Nizam. After returning from Indonesia, I had started working as Sub-Editor of this newspaper. When the Nizam banned the newspaper, it started publication from somewhere outside the state. In an article in this newspaper, the Nizam was severely criticized and his inhuman atrocities were reported with evidence. The article was written by a brilliant writer, Ramchandra Rao.

A true leader realizes the sufferings of others and tries to assuage these. In those days, every Arya Samaji used to be a true leader, that is why the Nizam was extremely angry to read the article and immediately passed an order to apprehend Ramchandra Rao dead or alive. His spies spread all over the state and finally on the information of an informer, Ramchandra Rao was arrested. He was produced in the Nizam's court and charged for sedition. The Judge ordered him to be whip-lashed a hundred times immediately.

Handcuffed, Ramchandra Rao was taken to the crossroad and as he received the first whip lash, Ramchandra uttered 'vandemataram'.

With the second whip-lash on his frail body, again there was a cry of 'vandemataram'. With each and every lash, he continued to utter 'vandemataram' vigorously. He was covered with blood, but his chanting of 'vandematarm' didn't stop.

After administrating 100 lashes, he was left at the roadside to die. But the moment, the Nizam's spies left him for dead, people lifted Ramchandra Rao on their shoulders and within no time, the crowd transformed into a freedom light procession. The popular youth leader, Narendra led this freedom procession and people blessed themselves with smearing their foreheads with the seeping blood of Ramchandra Rao. Hyderabad reverberated with the high pitch slogans, but the reverberating Vandemataram was not the word of Bankim Babu's Anandmath, but it had become a new name for Ramchandra Rao. He had become popular as Vandemataram. With the appearance of this news in the newspapers, groups of Arya Samaji demonstrators started pouring in from all parts of the country to Hyderabad and the background for freedom of Hyderabad was thus created. I resigned from the newspaper and prepared a plan to help the revolutionaries of the Arya

Samaj. In this connection, I started a florist shop and managed to make some people my clients, who used to take flowers for Hindu women in the palace or for Hindu Begums. The scheme paid off and I started getting secrets of the Nizam's schemes.

❑

31.

While preparations for the liberation of Hyderabad were underway, the army and Razakar goons had began their dirty mission of forcibly converting the majority of the Hindu population to Islam through intimidation and their atrocious ways. But most of the people were ready to die instead of renouncing their faith and they had to face the atrocities.

One day, while I and another woman near me were selling flowers, a horse-rider passed that way. On noticing a tilak on my forehead, he became furious and kicked our flower basket and whipped us badly and left with a warning of dire consequences, if we failed to embrace Islam and wear a burqa by the next day. He warned that he would come again and if his orders were not followed, he would flay us and take all our flowers.

Mehboobnagar, the changed name of Palmur, was known for the atrocities, but incidents of mass rape had made the town more wretched. Hundreds of Hindu girls and women were abducted from their homes. Barring Punjab, abduction of women on such a large scale had never been witnessed in recent history. After kidnapping, a Hindu girl would pass through forcible conversion to Islam and she was made to accompany the Muslim who held her hand, to live in his house or harem.

Vanisri, was 16-year-old daughter of a Hindu Zamindar (landlord). She was kidnapped and taken to the house of the Muslim Mukhiya of the village. First, she was gang-raped and then a person forced her to eat beef, thus defiled her dharma. That girl had never taken meat in her life. People present there laughed at her plight. She wept. In the meantime, a Mulla came there and recited some ayats of the Quran and forced her to recite these.

She was given a new name thereafter. Vani now was Zarina Bano. She was presented for bidding before the men of Markal village. The bid was won by a besta, i.e., a Muslim fisherman.

In Shadnagar also, there were conversions on a large scale and as a result, there were at least 3-4 women to a man in Muslim homes. As a result, males were idling their time in the houses or they would participate in the riots in the city, whereas the women would go outside earning their livelihood. In Umdanagar too, the name of which was later changed to Shamshabad, many Hindu women were gang-raped and Hindu houses were set on fire after mass murder of Hindus.

There were some such incidents, where in the name of riots, people took their personal revenge with people of their own community and religion. Such an incident took place at Kachiguda, where lingayat goons cornered a girl in the mid-street and gang raped her. Later it came to be known that the girl also belonged to a Lingayat family. Thus rioters have no religion. Rioters and rapists are neither Hindus nor Muslims, they are just oppressors and wicked. Even under such circumstances, I neither gave up selling flowers nor erased my tilak.

❑

32.

Revolutions are not created, they just arise due to circumstances. This, I had realized from the state of affairs in the state of Hyderabad. One day, there were no buyers for my flowers and I was sitting idle, I thought of reading something. I took out Satyarth Prakash and started reading it, when a young man stopped short seeing me reading. I then asked, "Brother, do you need flowers for your wife?"

"No, Amma, but I'll take flowers for her, but for now, a task.." he hesitated.

"So you are going to execute some work for her? It's nice to do something for her, but son, it's no wonder that we serve, but the thing is that it gives us pleasure. We must passionately undertake every task. Especially, we must try to fulfil every wish of the life partner."

"I do have the passion, Amma, but I'm not sure whether I would be able to accomplish it or not.."

"What do you want to do?"

"May I ask you one thing, Amma?"

"Yes"

"I think that you are an Arya Samaji."

"In fact, son, I consider the whole of India as a Samaj (community)."

"Then, you must have been protesting the atrocities, the Nizam has been heaping upon his subjects?"

"Who is not opposing these, son?"

"Will you do me a favour?"

"Tell me, son."

"In fact, I.."

"What I..? Tell me frankly."

"I want to meet the Nizam personally."

"Why?" I had become serious, "so, you too want to kill him?"

"What do you mean by you too? Who are the others who want to assassinate him?"

"Three boys, like you, had bombed his car, but he escaped."

"And, what did you do to protest against these atrocities?"

"I have been permitted to take flowers for Hindu Begums personally to King Kothi and Phalaknuma Palace, but that I had always been unable to find the wretched Nizam in his harem."

"Then, how do we locate him?"

"But, now since both of us have shaken hands, we are further strengthened. We will find him somehow." Then I asked that young man, "What is your name, son?

"Vaidhyanath."

"All right, next time, when he visits King Kothi for his amorous sport, I will soon arrange your meeting with the Hyderabad Nizam." I had promised him.

❑

33.

When, on 22 May, Razakars attacked the Hindus travelling in a train at Gangapur station, the Nehru government was criticized all over India for its soft corner for the Razakars, and for appeasement to Muslims, but there was a person, who didn't like this appeasement."

"Who was he, Amma?" I had asked Amma.

"Sardar Patel." Telling me, she continued with her narrative, "do you know how the plan to liberate Hyderabad was conceived?"

"How?"

"Then, listen!" She continued, as if she was bent upon sharing the entire history of independence.

But I had a feeling, she was left with very little time, that is why she wanted to download all her woes. Recounting the history, she...

Nehruji had asked Patel during a meeting, "Will it make any difference, if Hyderabad is not merged with India?"

Patel had replied, "If you are asked to guard the Anand Bhavan, will that make any difference?"

"What do you want to say?"

"I want total independence."

"Will it not be total independence minus Hyderabad?"

"No, it would be incomplete."

"Hyderabad had appealed to the United Nations to maintain its identity; would it not be interference in their internal affairs?"

"When his subjects have ruled him out, then who is he, what would he gain by appealing to the UN?"

"What do you mean by that his being ruled out by his subjects?"

"There has been a mass revolution under the Arya Samaj, which has laid the foundation stone for the merger. This mass revolution has blown up to the extent that a bomb has been lodged on the car of the Nizam. Being the Prime Minister, you, just allow us to take police action." Nehru was munching savouries, when Patel placed a paper before him and said, "we need your signature on this."

"What is this?

"It's a form for air ticket out of the PM's quota."

"Oh!" And without reading, Nehru signed the letter. In fact, it was not a request for an air ticket, but it was an order from the Prime Minister to take police action against Hyderabad. Patel, himself had typed that letter, because he knew that Nehru would not easily allow police action against Hyderabad.

❑

34.

Patel began Operation Polo on September 13, 1948 to attack Hyderabad. At 4 am in the morning, the Indian Army under the command of General Chaudhary entered Hyderabad from five points. The Nizam's forces provided mild resistance, but they were defeated and almost 400 Razakars were made prisoners. Rizvi was also arrested from a rest house at the bank of the lake. The Nizam announced a truce on 18th September and invited the Indian Army to Sikandrabad and the Razakars were banned. When the Nizam's Chief of Army Staff, General Aldros placed his sword at the feet of the Indian Army Chief, General Chaudhary, Patel departed for Hyderabad.[27]

Sketch: Chief of the Hyderabad State and Former Nizam Osman Ali with Sardar Patel

❑

35.

When Hyderabad merged with India, I was released from the Palmur Jail and later I came to know that Vaidyanath was thrown into the jungle for dead, but he died later at the hospital. I too was jailed for helping him to reach the personal chamber of the Nizam. He had died, but I was unfortunate, that I could not die. I was tortured in the Nizam's jail, but these atrocities were far less than the implemented treatment met out to Vaidyanath. My hands were tied with a chain fixed in the wall and was whipped badly. They wanted to know, if we were sent by the Government of India to assassinate the Nizam, but that had never been the case. I was offered a number of allurements in the form of money, land, etc., in return for my accepting that I was sent by the Government of India to assassinate the Nizam, but neither had I any interest for these allurements, nor was I a traitor, so I was not prepared to give any false statement, come what may. Anyway, I was released only after the liberation of Hyderabad. Somehow, I reached the village of Vaidyanath, where I heard about Savitri performing sati.."

"Savitri performing Sati...meaning..!"

❑

36.

This story unfolds at Narkatiaganj in Champaran district. Savitri had come to this village after her marriage. Vaidyanath was her husband and her father-in-law was Dharichhanram.[28] At the time of marriage, Vaidyanath was 19 years and Savitri was at the tender age of 15 years. She had not attained womanhood, even then her mother-in-law had sent her with a glass of milk for the first night of the couple's union.

"Please drink the milk." Veiled Savitri had said.

"No, keep it on the stool and come to me."

"No..no..I won't come to you."

"Why? We are a legally married couple, you have not eloped with me, you would be mother to our children." Saying this, he had begun to fondle her.

"I don't want to be mother of Muslim children in this enslaved country," she had withdrawn from him. She was unaware of the ways of life, but she believed that just by touching a woman with lips, she gets pregnant.

"Mother of Muslim children in this enslaved country? What are you saying, Savitri?"

"I am telling the truth, I have listened to bhajans of Bastiram Agniban. He had said that the Nizam of Hyderabad is converting all Hindus to Islam, saying that the Mughals would once again rule from Kashmir to Kanyakumari and would convert all Hindus into Muslims. No, I don't want to be converted to Islam and eat meat, nor would I give birth to meat-eater children. He had banned the Ved mantras also. I love Ved mantras, not the ajan."

"Then what would you do?"

"I am a woman, what can I do, it is you who have to act."

"And, what should I do?"

"Go and behead the Nizam, so that our children can be saved and they could fearlessly recite Ved mantras."

"Do you think, it is that simple?"

"Then go and get your head severed, I would take pride in dying as the widow of a martyr than that of a coward."

So, the 19-year-old youth, Vaidyanath had immediately left for Hyderabad on his mission. He managed to get information about the Nizam being present at King Kothi on that day and avoiding the prying eyes, he reached there. Not even that, he had managed to reach the chamber of the Nizam with a dagger and hide under his bed. The whimsical Nizam entered the room with 2-3 women, whom he ordered to make a search of the room.

Vaidyanath was caught. He was taken to a jail in the jungles of Palmur, where he was heavily tortured. He was induced to accept Islam, but he didn't yield and firmly adhered to his faith.

The irritated jailer had asked him, "What is your problem? What objection do you have in accepting Islam?"

"I have no objection, but my wife has. She wants the severed head of the Nizam."

"Leave that wife and adopt Islam. You would be married to a most beautiful woman. I'll get you married to my sister-in-law and you would be provided wealth and property."

"Now, you tell me, jailer, how could I leave an innocent woman, who has sacrificed her life, her husband for the cause of her nation and her faith?" Vaidyanath had replied.

He was tortured to the extent that he had reached the verge of death, which was inevitable, as he subjected to implement treatment, for he was forced to sit on a chair which had a long pointed nail at the centre of the seat, which must have pierced his anus and reached his lungs in the body. That is why he was taken for dead and his body thrown in the jungle. When he was spotted by some Hindus, he was alive. He was taken far away from the Nizam state to Betia hospital, where he was admitted and he breathed his last on June 25, 1948.[29]

The dead body was brought to his native village, where everyone wept bitterly, but Savitri had no tears in her eyes. Women started whispering, what a wretched widow she is, she is not in the least grieved at the death of her husband. Her bangles had been smashed. Then Savitri took off all the jewellery she was wearing, went into the house, took out the remaining jewellery kept in the house and said to her father-in-law, "Father, all of you must be very sad at the death of my husband, but I am very happy, as I have sacrificed him for the country and the faith. Will you fulfil my last wish?"

"Tell me, beti."

"Please accept these ornaments and sell them and with the proceeds, kindly make a pilgrim house and a yajnashala." She was in the process of handing over the ornaments, when she bowed to touch the feet of her father-in-law, but couldn't and fell at his feet. Some of the women picked her up but, she was no more. Both the husband and wife were placed on a single pyre and funeral rites were carried out. Wooden sticks and flames had hidden their bodies. That night or rather the first night of union of the couple was darkness amidst light for them. In due course a pilgrim house was built in the memory of the martyr, Vaidyanath, but the inscription didn't mention Savitri.[30]

❑

37.

"Amma! Didn't you return to your village?" I had asked her.

"Like Bhamashah, father had sold his entire property and along with the proceeds, he had offered my brother Basant Kumar to Netaji for the cause of the country. Later, my brother had renounced the world and had become a recluse. There was a time, when we had a large business at Calcutta," Amma had started telling her story, "but I loved my native village, where I had spent my golden years of childhood. I had visited my village after the Hyderabad Liberation Movement, but my family members refused to recognize me and said, 'She can't be Neera, must be a cheat or trickster. Neera was killed by Srikant and it was thereafter that Srikant was killed by the soldiers of Azad Hind. Neera had taken birth in a country, where women performed sati with their husbands, but this sinful woman became the cause of her husband's death.' I went to the Arya Samaj temple of the village, whose chairman was a chamar (cobbler) Yadram and treasurer was a bania (merchant) Mahavir Prasad Gupta. I had requested them for a room to stay at the Arya Samaj temple, which they had refused. Mahavir Prasad had known my family well and he had recognized me in the beginning, but when I expressed my desire to stay in the village, suddenly he refused to recognize me."[31]

"I went to Bawali village (Near Baraut) also, which was 20-25 kilometres from my village, where I met Chaudhary Karan Singh Tomar, who had served in the INA and he too was taken to Cellular Jail by the same ship, in which I had travelled. He had also participated in the Indo-China war of 1962. He gave me a patient hearing and said, "Sister, stay with me at my house, it will be my privilege."

"But I can't be a burden on anybody."

"Then don't expect anything from the government or society," he said. "I was in the INA, then I served the Jat Regiment, but during this period of distress, I am wandering from door to door to get a certificate of dependence on a freedom struggle for my son."

I was shocked to listen to Karan Singh's talk which is why people do not respect freedom fighters, why they don't get the honour they deserve.

❑

38.

"Indira Gandhi was Prime Minister in those days and she had honoured freedom fighters, why didn't you meet her? She would have helped you, you could have got a pension and government accommodation too."

"You are very simple, beti, Farhana Taj!"

"What happened, Amma?"

"Whatever I did for the country, it was never for getting honoured or for pension in my old age. Why do I need a government accommodation, when the entire country is mine, I can reside wherever I want. The country has now attained independence. While fighting for the independence, we never dreamt of becoming a leader or leading a life of comfort."

"Then? Weren't you disappointed with the behaviour of people of your village? What did you think in those days?"

"I never had any expectations from the villagers. In fact, those are fortunate, who really love others from their hearts. They are small people, they are insignificant, but they are fortunate. Everything depends on how we love each other. Hatred or condemnation by others has no meaning for me, as I had been made to love human beings, because we are all vanshaj of Aryan. Yet, I was disappointed in my village, but disappointment leads you nowhere, as it is the outcome of foolishness. It has the same effect on one's soul that is visible at the time of catastrophic floods in the people. I was refused shelter even in the Arya Samaj Mandir, which was built on the land that my father donated at the time of my birth...

"As that was not enough, I thought of seeking a job at the Saraswati Library, which was established in 1935 by my father in Khekra, which housed rare books and manuscripts. But, when I tried to locate the library, I failed...when asked, some people told me that the library was built on a disputed land and now a market had come up on the land and the library was shifted with a new name of Sri Gandhi Library to a room in Mahavir Jain Dharmshala, near the Khekra police post. It was known as Janata Library. The Dharmshala management had also pressurized to vacate the room, where the library was housed, but what happened to those rare books and manuscripts, was not known. The only information that could be found was that the library might have auctioned them to pay for the rent and a public school had bought some books in that auction. But I am surprised, how can a person sell the government books of the library which had been receiving subsidy and books from the government's Raja Ram Mohan Roy Library of Calcutta. I wondered about how many such government libraries might have been sold by greedy people just for occupying the land. What an independence! What a Government of India! Did we suffer torture in the jails to see such days? Should we have expected a comfortable life in lieu of the atrocities that we faced? But how could I know about comfort, when my entire youth had been spent in jail.

As such, I thought of going to jail, instead of imploring some leaders to get facilities."

"What could you achieve by going to jail in independent India?"

"I was nearing the end of my journey in the world. I came to Delhi by train without a ticket. I had thought that I would be caught travelling without a ticket by the TT and put in jail and the rest of my life would pass comfortably in the jail. In the jail also, I would not remain idle, as the jail authorities extract work from the inmates, which is more worthwhile than the food they provide. The outside environment, too, was no better than a jail for me! Streets were still unsafe for a woman at midnight in independent India. If a person avoids helping other hungry, thirsty, ill or a helpless person, then in fact, he is dishonouring the call of God. People of Khekra were also acting in this manner.

"I had to spend my youth in jail, but now that bloody TT didn't ask for my ticket, I got down at Shahdara and took another local train, thought now I would have been caught travelling without a ticket, but my bad luck, I was not checked. I alighted at Nizamuddin station and I boarded another train and took my seat in the last compartment, thinking this must be a long route train, I would definitely be caught and would be jailed, where I could live peacefully, but for 36 hours the train stopped at a number of stations, and several TT came to the compartment, during the 36 hours of journey of that fast moving train, but none of them asked for my ticket. I lay there hungry in a ragged condition, but nobody asked either for the ticket or if I was hungry. I was not a beggar, so I didn't beg anybody. Ultimately, I reached Namapally station, returning once again to the area, familiar to me. Once again, I started selling flowers for ladies' braids..and thus started earning my livelihood. I couldn't realize, when my bones had become so frail. Now, I had gone beyond the feeling of joy or pain. There are only two states in life, which are painful, one, when one's wishes are fulfilled and second, when wishes remain unfulfilled. My wishes had not been fulfilled, as the country had not attained the real independence and my wishes were not unfulfilled too, as the country had now been liberated. I had never liked to nurse my wishes, as I had only one desire and that was to see my country independent and that desire had been fulfilled. I, however, felt that the least desires, one has the more he or she is happy. A person who is devoid of wishes, would always be happy and I wanted to leave this world with a smile on my face."

All of a sudden, she had a violent hiccup and her mouth was agape and her eyes were stationary. My fiancé ran for the doctor and the doctor felt her pulse and said, "Sorry, she is no more! Please pay the bill, then only will you be able to take her."[32] She had died, but it was hard to believe.

❑

39.

I was not related to Amma through blood, but I felt as if my heart was sinking and I had became emotionally charged. I tried hard, but couldn't stop tears coming from my eyes. My fiancé had gone to settle the hospital bill and getting the discharge papers. After completing the formalities, he came back and said, "First of all, her dead body will have to be removed from the hospital, but where to take her and how to cremate her? I'll take her to my room, but the hospital authorities have refused to provide an ambulance and advised me to get the ambulance from outside..so I am going to make an arrangement for a tempo." He left leaving me alone by the side of Amma. The wait was endless and he had not returned. In the meantime, the hospital staff was pestering me to remove the dead body immediately. They had wrapped her in a white cloth, the bed was to be vacated, I tried hard to convince them that my fiancé had gone for a vehicle, they said to me, "You don't know. She is not related to him, he is from Delhi and must have ran away leaving you with the dead body. You brought her to the hospital, got her admitted and put your name on the papers as the daughter of this lady. Now don't tell lies, you are her real daughter, her illegitimate child of old age...take her away."

"No, he will come..she was from his village..and he had sold his gold medal for her treatment only yesterday..that was

the only gold medal he had received in his life and that too was sold by him for her treatment..she is related to him, not to me...please allow me to wait for him, then we will take her.."

"Will you take this dead body or else..."

They were talking nonsense and had started pulling the dead body by its leg and as I said, "Please handle her gently." They lifted Amma and placed the body on my shoulder...I had shouted, "Oh! what are you doing? Why are you putting the dead body on my shoulder?"

"It is your Amma, take her away, otherwise we will throw you out with her also."

I took Amma in my lap, but by lifting the dead body, my waist got jolted, though she was not that heavy, the soul had left the body for heaven. Crying bitterly, I managed to come out of the hospital lifting her dead body in my lap with great difficulty and as I stepped out, I saw an auto stopping near me and my fiancé got out of it and said, "Why have you brought her like this?"

"She is my mother, Mother India.." I said with a choked throat. My fiancé took Amma in his arms and got into the auto, I also sat beside him and asked the auto driver to take us to his rented house. The auto started, it was running fast on the road. Suddenly, the driver looked back and sighting the dead body wrapped in a white cloth he exclaimed, "Oh! it's a dead body...put her away...I do not take dead bodies in my auto..you have defiled my auto..." and he stopped the auto and pulled my fiancé out, but during this scuffle, Amma was about to fall on the ground...Oh! she would get hurt," I cried.

"Does a dead body get hurt?" the auto driver said. My family and I were standing on the road at midnight with the dead body of Amma. Those who dedicate their lives for the cause of society, do not care for their fame. Such was the personality of Amma, she too had no concern about her dead body.

There was no alternative for us, but to carry the body manually to our room.

We put her on a sheet on the floor, but as we were laying her, I felt as Amma had a hiccup. Overjoyed, I cried, "Amma is alive!"

My fiancé too was astonished, but he pulled his face and just nodded. Then he brought sacred Ganges water and poured it in her mouth. A few drops got inside her mouth and some fell on the ground. But the nectar of the sacred Ganges could not revive her. My fiancé went outside the room and brought some dry sticks and made a fire. In the meanwhile, some members of my family also reached there looking for me. They too were saddened to hear about Amma's death. They were also astonished to see us doing so much for a stranger. But it was hard to make them realize that she was not a stranger, but she was the person, who was instrumental in getting independence for us. We often fear sacrifice, which we are to make. But where there is love, sacrifice is also there, happiness and peace also prevail there. This is what I had learned from Amma.

❑

40.

It was daybreak, birds were chirping and some people were preparing a bier for Amma's last journey. Amma was a Hindu, as such my fiancé wanted to perform her last rites as per Hindu customs with pure ghee and other material, he had no money and the local shopkeeper had refused to provide material on credit. Therefore, without informing my family, I gave the golden ring to him, which had been gifted to me by him. He had gone for making arrangements for a canister of ghee for last rites by pawning the ring. Preparation for Amma's funeral procession had been completed, people were just waiting for my fiancé to arrive. He must have been stuck somewhere. I was also waiting for him, when suddenly it occurred to me that Amma was a true nationalist, as such she deserved the honour that a patriot or a martyr gets. I just got up and started for a nearby school, where the morning prayer was over and all the students had departed for their classes. I somehow managed to pull down the tricolor, but I was spotted by the guard, who started shouting, 'Thief, thief!'

Before people could realize the situation, I sprinted towards the rented house and I had no time to look back. Breathless, I reached the house, when I saw that people were just lifting the bier, I was there in time to cover the body with the tricolour. People present there, looked at me with bewildered eyes, but none of them said anything and they had lifted the bier on their shoulder and started for the cremation ground. At that moment, a jeep halted there and the principal and the peon along with two constables alighted from the jeep and pointing to me, the peon said, "This is the woman who had dishonoured the national flag and had stolen the school flag and God knows, what other things she might have stolen. I know her and her lover well, I have seen both of them in this house in objectionable positions. I knew that the thief would be there." He was addressing the policemen and was boasting about himself and was narrating my untold story, of which even I was not aware. In fact, if we want to love, then we must also learn to forgive others. I, therefore, ignored all these allegations, as I was filled with grief over the death of Amma and I had tears in my eyes. But the peon was unaware of the real situation, so he said, "Look at the thief, who is weeping for the fear of being caught." The constables had put me in the jeep and the jeep had started moving. Sobbing, I looked back, Amma was moving away from me to a distant, a far distant place, probably for a new spy mission or for lighting a torch of liberation for some other nation, for which she had been offering herself to the flames! Suddenly, the sky became clouded and the day had turned dark and then it started raining followed by thunder. Rain drops fell on the ground, as if God was also giving Amma a tearful farewell![33]

Om Shanti Om

References and Remarks

1. Only a few days before my marriage, I came to know about my fiancé being a non-Muslim, while my family came to know of it only after the marriage and it had caused turmoil not only in my mind, but also in the family and in our society. I have written about this in my book '*Mera Doosra Janma*' (My Second Birth).

2. A gentleman, Begraj, an Aryan preacher was the first to write a narrative poem on Neera Arya. He used to sing lyrics based on Neera at the meetings of the Arya Samaj. In 1988, a resident of village Dhikoli, a senior military officer of the Indian National Army narrated the whole story of Neera Arya in his speech at the annual function of the Khekra Arya Samaj. Tejpal Singh Dhama was among the audience, who inspired by his speech, wrote the first story about Neera, '*Lal Kile par sone ka Khekra*', which was published in the local daily '*Samagra Samachar*', '*Baraut Toofani*', and Baraut monthly magazine, '*Khas ka Jhad*' and soon it became the talk of the town. Nemchand Bhagirathi Saini Rama was the editor of '*Khas ka Jhad*' and '*Baraut Toofani*' and had his office at the bank of the canal near the Baraut

Railway Station. He serialized the story of Neera in the weekly magazine, *Baraut Toofani*.

3. *Bhooli Bisari Aitihasik Kahnian*, by Tejpal Singh Dhama, Surya Bharati Prakashan, Chawri Bazar, Delhi, 2014 edition, p. 78.

4. *Guamnam Krantikari*, Sagar Prakashan, 2003 edition, p. 57.

5. *Jivan Sangharsha*, Gunmala Somani, Hindi Sahitya Sadan, DB Gupta Road, Karol Bagh, New Delhi, 2004 edition, p. 60.

6. In a number of books, Mahavir has been mentioned as the real father of Neera, whereas Jute King, Chhajjumal (Chhajjuram) was his godfather, who had adopted her. Chhajjumal was born on November 27, 1865 in a Jat family of *Lamba gotra* of Chaudhary Saligram in Alakhpura village of Bhawanikhera Tehsil in today's Bhiwani District. His childhood was spent in poverty, struggles and misfortune, but with his hard work, perseverance and resolve, he reached the pinnacle of success. He was appointed director of the Punjab National Bank, but due to excessive work duties, he resigned. At one time, Chhajjuram's assets had crossed 40 million marks. There was a time, when he didn't have money to buy an umbrella, but now he was among the richest merchants of the country. He constructed his 21 bungalows in Calcutta (14 Alipur, 7 Bara Bazar). GD Birla and Lala Lajpat Rai, the lion of Punjab had been the tenants of Chaudhary Chhajjuramji. He got a palatial bungalow constructed at Alakhpura (Hansi), got constructed the Arya Samaj building at Khekra, a village of Uttar Pradesh and adopted two children of

the village, named Neera Arya and her brother Basant Kumar. He also purchased five villages in Haryana and 1,600 bighas of land in Bhiwani, Hissar and Sheikhpura of Bhawanikhera, Alipura, Alakhpura, Kumharon ki Dhani, Kagsar, Jamni, Khandakheri and Moth villages. He also owned peanut oil extraction plants. In those days, a few rajas owned Rolls Royce cars, but his elder son had this car.

7. '*Hukke se Haq tak*' by Dr. Ranjit Singh, p. 32.

8. बोस इसी साड़ी ल्यादे हो, जिसकी चमक निराली
बोस इसी साड़ी ल्यादे हो, जिसकी चमक निराली
साड़ी ऊपर फोटू केमा, भारत के सभी आर्य हों
तिलक गोखले ऋषि दयानंद स्वामी शंकराचार्य हों
गौरमिंट जहाँ उस दिल्ली मै राजगोपालाचार्य हों
रक्षा मंत्री भारत के बलदेव सिंह सरदार भी हों
राजेंद्रप्रसाद पटेल गांधी वीर जवाहर भी हों
हँसते-हँसते जेलों अंदर पड़ने को तैयार भी हों
काले पानी पहुँचाए जिन्होंने जान खपाली
बोस इसी साड़ी ल्यादे हो, जिसकी चमक निराली
चंद्रशेखर वीर भगत सिंह रास बिहारी बोस भी हों
लाला लाजपतराय लाहौर मै पिटते हुए निर्दोष भी हों
राजगुरु सुखदेव व बिस्मिल मरते हुए मै जोश भी हो
जलियांवाले बाग का जलसा, डायर फायर करता हो
भारत का बदला लेने लंदन मै शोर बिचरता हो
ऊधम सिंह की गोली सै लंदन मै डायर मरता हो
डायर मारा आप मरा गया ना वार कति खाल्ली
बोस इसी साड़ी ल्यादे हो, जिसकी चमक निराली
राम और लक्ष्मण राज छोड़कै बण में धक्के खाते हों
हरिश्चंद्र भी सत्य के कारण काशी में बिक जाते हों

Source: Dinanath Vyas Kavyalankar, August sun 42 ka Mahan Viplav (Agra, 1946); India Unreconciled published by Hindustan Times Press (Delhi, 1943); Reports of Enquiry Committees appointed by the Provincial and the District Congress Committees and Provincial Governments; National Herald (Lucknow, 1946); Aaj (Kashi, 1946); Daily Sansar (Kashi, 1946); Abhyudaya (Allahabad, 1946); NAI Home Poll. F.No. 3/79/42, 1942.

जगदेव पँवार काटकै गर्दन दान मै शीश चढ़ाते हों?
मोर धवज भी चीर कै लड़का करसन का शोर जिमाते हों
हिरणाकुश प्रहलाद भक्त को लाल खंभ पकड़ाते हों
राजा भोज बिक्रमादित्य प्रजा का कष्ट मिटाते हों
दिन आजादी का हो, मिलके सब पूजै दीवाली
बोस इसी साड़ी ल्यादे हो, जिसकी चमक निराली
रामायण महाभारत गीता धार्मिक इतिहास भी हो
आजादी आती दिखै और गुलामी का नाश भी हो
लालकिले पै तिरंगा झंडा, सामने खड़ा सुभाष भी हो
सरदार सिंह तूफान कह गुरु पृथ्वी सिंह उमंग मै हों
मजदूर किसानों का सेवक सर छोटू राम भी संग मै हों
भारत माँ का बच्चा बच्चा इस आजादी की जंग में हों
साँकरोद के नक्शे में सब दिखैं हाली-पाली
बोस इसी साड़ी ल्यादे हो, जिसकी चमक निराली

9. In 1982, at a function organized in the memory of Neera at Khekra cowshed, a saint had participated, about whom it was claimed that he was Netaji Subhas Chandra Bose. During the days of his youth, Tejpal Singh Dhama was a witness to that programme, but in his speech, the saint had denied his being Netaji. Chaudhary Begraj of Patti Mundala told him that he had seen Netaji Subhas in 1942 and he quite resembled Netaji. When he said he felt that he was Subhas, the saint smiled and said, "Netaji's one hand was slightly smaller than the other one, but look at my hands, which do not differ in size. As such, I am not Netaji Subhas." That saint had been living in Faizabad in those days and was known as '*Gumnami baba*' (An unknown saint). In 1955, when he died, a number of articles were found in his belongings, which were related to Netaji Subhas Chandra Bose. Sardar Singh Toofan had sung '*Bose aisi saree Lyade...*' *ragini* before him.

Later, at a grand function organized by Tejpal Singh Dhama, he sought blessings of all the freedom fighters of the Baghpat District. At that function, Sardar Singh Toofan once again rendered his popular *ragini* and said that he had sung this *ragini* on All India Radio a number of times. A group photo of this function has also been included in this book.

10. *Azad Hind ke Gumnam Krantikari*, by Manmathnath Gupta, Hind Pocket Books, GT Road, Shahadara, Dellhi-32, 1966 edition, p. 97.

11. *Bhoole Bisare Krantikari*, Tejpal Singh Dhama, Gyan Ganga Prakashan, Shahdara

12. कदम कदम बढ़ाए जा, खुशी के गीत गाये जा
ये जिंदगी है कौम की, तू कौम पे लुटाये जा
तू शेर-ए-हिन्द आगे बढ़, मरने से तू कभी न डर
उड़ा के दुश्मनों का सर, जोश-ए-वतन बढ़ाये जा
हिम्मत तेरी बढ़ती रहे, खुदा तेरी सुनता रहे
जो सामने तेरे खड़े, तू खाक में मिलाये जा
चलो दिल्ली पुकार के, कौमी-निशाँ संभाल के
लाल किले पे गाड़ के, लहराये जा लहराये जा

13. *Azad Hind ke Gumnam Krantikari*, by Manmathnath Gupta, Hind Pocket Books, Shahadara, Dellhi-32, 1966, p. 112.

14. *Kale Paani ka Kaharnama*, page 58.

15. सरफरोशी की तमन्ना अब हमारे दिल में है,
देखना है जोर कितना बाजु-ए-कातिल में है।
रहरवे राहे-मुहब्बत रह न जाना राह में,
लज्जते सहरा-नवर्दी दूरि-ए-मंजिल में है।।
अब न अगले वलवले हैं और न अरमानों की भीड़,

अब तो मिट जाने की हसरत इक दिले बिस्मिल में है।
आज मकतल में यह कातिल कह रहा है बार-बार,
क्या भला शौके शहादत भी किसी के दिल में है?
वक्त आने दे बता दूँगा तुझे ए आसमाँ
हम अभी से क्या बताएँ क्या हमारे दिल में है।
ऐ शहीदे, मुल्को मिल्लत मैं तेरे ऊपर निसार
अब तेरी हिम्मत का चर्चा गैर की महफिल में है।

16. मिट गया जब मिटने वाला फिर सलाम आया तो क्या?
दिल की बरबादी के बाद उनका पयाम आया तो क्या?
काश अपनी जिंदगी में हम य' मंजर देखते,
यूँ सरे तुरबत कोई महशरखराम आया तो क्या?
मिट गई जुमला उमीदें, जाता रहा सारा खयाल,
उस घड़ी फिर नामाबर पयाम लेकर आया तो क्या?
ऐ दिले नाकाम मिट जा अब तो कूचे यार में
फिर मेरी नाकामियों के बाद काम आया तो क्या?
आखिरी शब दीद के काबिल थी बिस्मिल की तड़प
सुबह दम गर कोई भी बालाए बाम आया तो क्या?

17. हाय जननी जन्मभूमि छोड़कर जाते हैं हम, देखना फिर कब वापस लौटकर आते हैं हम

18. Recounting his experiences in his book, '*Bandi Jeevan*', Shachindranath Sanyal has presented a similar description, as told by Neera.

19. A number of other authors have expressed similar views, as such it can be said that men and women were subjected to similar punishments.

20. R. L. Sharma had underwent somewhat similar incidents.

21. Memoirs of Ramcharanlal Sharma also resemble the experiences of Neera. Neera, however, has been the editor of R. L. Sharma's book and she has described

incidents related to her under the pretext of Ramcharanlal. She could not write all this in her own name for the fear of disgrace.

22. *'Kale Paani ka Kaharnama'*, Ramcharanlal Sharma, Atmaram & Sons, Delhi-6, p. 79.

23. *Angrezo ka Bhartiya Nari par Kahar*, R.P. Sharma, p. 82.

24. *Azad Hind ke Gumnam Krantikari*, by Manmathnath, p. 136.

25. Savarkar has also described the eating of oysters by the aboriginals of Andaman, which is similar to the description given by Neera. Please look at p. 229.

26. '*Bhagyanagar ka Quaidi'*, Tejpal Dhama, p. 12.

27. *Lovelorn Begum and Lost Nizam*, Farhana Taj, Sagar Publcations, Shahadara, Delhi-32, 2015 edition, p. 160.

28. '*Arya Samaj ke Mahadhan, Swami Swatantrananda*', Publisher – Arya Pratinidhi Sabha Ramlila Ground, Delhi, 1948 edition, p. 266.

29. *Ibid*.

30. '*Ved Vraksha ki Chhaya Talay*', Farhana Taj, Dhama Sahitya Sadan, Shahadara, Delhi, 2015 edition, p. 294.

31. '*Agnichakra*', Tejpal Singh Dhama, Publisher – Yuva Vikas Parishad, UP, 2001 edition, p. 204

32. '*Ghar Vapasi*', Farhana Taj, Urdu, first edition 2003, p.29.

33. As a godson, co-author, Tejpal Singh Dhama performed '*mukhagni'* for Neera.

❑